Practical Yoga

ANCIENT AND MODERN

BY ERNEST E. WOOD

MIND AND MEMORY TRAINING

OCCULT TRAINING OF THE HINDUS

AN ENGLISHMAN DEFENDS MOTHER INDIA

GARUDA PURANA

TEXTBOOK OF CITIZENSHIP

PRACTICAL YOGA: ANCIENT AND MODERN

Practical Yoga

ANCIENT AND MODERN

By Ernest E. Wood

*Being a new, independent translation of
Patanjali's Yoga Aphorisms,
interpreted in the light of ancient and modern
psychological knowledge and practical experience*

With an introduction by Paul Brunton

1973 EDITION

Published by
WILSHIRE BOOK COMPANY
12015 Sherman Road
No. Hollywood, California 91605
Telephone: (213) 875-1711

Printed by

HAL LEIGHTON PRINTING CO.
P. O. Box 1231
Beverly Hills, California 90213
Telephone: (213) 346-8500

ISBN 0-87980-149-2

CONTENTS

Introduction by Paul Brunton

Practical Yoga

ANCIENT AND MODERN

E·P·DUTTON & CO. INC
1852 1953
CREATIVE · IOI YEARS · PUBLISHING

INTRODUCTION

By
PAUL BRUNTON
Author of *A Search in Secret India*

The little information we have about Patanjali is legendary and not trustworthy. Scholars have different opinions as to the date when he lived and worked, varying by as much as several centuries. But the most commonly accepted date is the second century B.C. Indeed he is regarded by most Hindus themselves as identical with the celebrated grammarian of the same name, who belonged to that period.

Patanjali did not originate yoga. It is known to have existed long before his time. Yajnavalkya, who lived at least a thousand years before him, enjoined in his writings the duty of retirement into the forests at a certain age, for the practice of religious devotion and mystic contemplation. Yoga was also briefly touched upon in other earlier books, such as *The Maitri Upanishad*. What Patanjali did was to collect the experiences, the knowledge and the opinions of some other yogis and align them with his own. He then formulated definite principles and a precise teaching out of them and summarized them in a short text, which has become a classical authority in its homeland. It is also needful to remember that he belonged to a particular school, the Raja-Yog, whereas there were several others. There are today at least eleven other known schools, whilst in my researches and travels I discovered quite a few little-known secret schools.

Patanjali's meanings are somewhat obscure at times. His style makes for difficult reading. He is incredibly concise. Even Indians have felt and told me this. A commentary by a competent person is indispensable. The most celebrated was written by Vyasa. Both Patanjali and Vyasa were several years ago rendered, in a scholarly translation, from the original Sanskrit into English in the

9

Harvard Oriental Series, but the difficulties remain. Only those who know from actual experience what they read about in the text can really understand Patanjali. This is because whereas other Indians sought truth by intellectual logic, Patanjali sought it by intellect-transcending meditation. Moreover, like so many other early mystical and philosophical Indian writings, his were primarily intended for the use of teachers rather than for the use of students. They were really a series of subject-headings of which explanations could be given personally and lectures could be delivered vocally. They are extremely difficult for the modern reader to follow coherently. Hence a modern commentary for contemporary students is necessary, and Professor Wood has filled that need in his most readable work. Moreover there is definitely a place for the new translation which he offers. While faithful to the original, it is more flexible than earlier ones. Professor Wood has practiced yoga and is well qualified to write reliably on the subject. He has lived in India for the span of a whole generation and has an adequate knowledge of the Sanskrit language.

Aphorisms on Yoga is the title which Patanjali gave his work. The term "yoga" is used in Hindu literature in different senses. In the art of arithmetic, yoga means addition, but in astronomy it is a technical term while in religion it means something else still. But the general sense always remains the same, and that is: a unification of two or more diverse elements, a whole which includes or unites several parts. In Patanjali's specific sense, it is the establishment of perfect harmony between the everyday self and its spiritual source. It is what we in the Western hemisphere often call mysticism.

Yoga, in this sense, became the basis of one of the six classical systems of traditional Hindu philosophy. But it is really independent of any particular revealed religion and is to be found in the records of all revealed religions. The true mystic may belong to the Christian church, the Hindu temple or the Muhameddan mosque, if he wishes.

In the Old Testament, the yogic condition is concisely indicated by the frequently used phrase, "and the Spirit of the Lord (Jehovah) came upon him," as the yogic method is correctly described by the Psalmist's "Be still and know that I am God." In the Chris-tion fold something like yoga has been always practiced. Christianity has, throughout its long history, held a mystical element. Not a few men among the early anchorites round the Mediterranean shores, some of the women in medieval Catholic convents, and entire Quaker communities in the United States of America learnt to sit in meditation. It is not really something exotic and entirely alien to the West; it is only a neglected and a half-forgotten art. Yoga, if stripped of its Hinduistic forms, its legendary histories, would be quite at home in a Christian framework. We shall understand Joan of Arc better if we can understand that her phenomena were symptoms of one kind of yogic state into which she fell involuntarily at times.

The yogi achieves the ultimate in passivity, the extreme in self-absorption. His ecstatic state may be brought about by a variety of means, lower or higher, physical or mental. He may whirl his body around like an Egyptian dervish, and fall into ecstasy at the end. Or he may sit immobile, austere and uncommunicative, like the man whose cave on a hill overlooking the Arabian Sea I visited a couple of years ago. Some Indians hold their breath for as long as they can, others hold their feet twisted behind their back, still others disdain all such gymnastics and plunge straightway into holding their mind on one subject—the true self as the object of their search.

Three quarters of a century ago, Tylor showed, in his *Primitive Culture,* that savage tribes of the earliest antiquity greatly esteemed the ecstatic condition, which they induced by meditation, fasting or narcotics. The shamans of Siberia and Mongolia, the medicine-men of North America and the wizards of Polynesia—among many others—sought and found this condition. But they did so rarely for its own sake, more often for the sake of the abnormal psychological and physical phenomena which were its byproducts. They wanted to see into the future, be impervious to wounds, obtain guidance for their fellow tribesmen from above or communicate by telepathy over long distances, and so on.

An unfortunate result of this is that there are some people, both among the modern Indians themselves and among the Western missionaries who have worked in India, to whom the name yoga carries sinister connotations of witchcraft, sorcery and black magic. That there are men addicted to these horrible pursuits is unfortunately a fact. That they are not followers of Patanjali's yoga is however equally a fact. For the reader will see that a whole section is devoted by Patanjali to the regime of moral self-purification which, according to him, must precede the practices of meditation exercises. Indeed a warning is needed here that such exercises should be let alone if the character is too sunk in weakness, in sin or in evil. The celebrated German occultist, Rudolf Steiner, rightly pointed out that for every step taken in mystical development, three steps should be taken in moral development. Let no one mistake fantastic notions and superstitious customs for the true yoga. Let no one seek the merely incidental strange phenomena of mysticism to feed his spiritual hunger. The phenomena may be real or pretended, but the end result will be the same—spiritual starvation.

Among more advanced peoples an aim and a technique like Patanjali's were the most respected. Today only the higher means should be used and only the higher goals should be sought. Indeed, impure seeking can find no other result than incorrect vision. In the best school, that of philosophic yoga, the pupil has first to subject himself to a discipline which will not only separate him from the weaknesses and evils in his character but will also throw off the emotional prejudices and egoistic bias which prevent making his approach to truth as impersonal as any scientist's.

The true yogic state is one of mental exaltation reflecting an ardent communion with the divine. He who enters it discovers the mentalness of 'here' and 'there,' 'then' and 'to be,' and thus claims his freedom from an ancient tyrant. He begins to live in the timeless Now as he begins to live in the tranquillity of the spiritual mind. He realizes that Infinite Duration as opposed to finite time is always with him: he is always in it. In this sense he is immortal. But the 'he' here concerned is not the lower part of human nature. The more the lower self persists in clinging to the finite sense of time's passage, the more it prevents entry into the very deathlessness which it desires. To those who have never reflected about it, there is something incomprehensible and even uncanny in the idea, but those who have done so know that there is noble power and satisfying peace in it. How much more must it mean to those who can reach its beautiful shores and sit brooding over its infinite depths!

We do not have to know much about the body's anatomy to know that an infinitely wise intelligence betrays itself therein and that atheism is absurd. We do not have to know much about the mind's anatomy either to reach the same conclusion. But whereas a few days in the dissecting room of a medical college may be enough to reach it by the first way, fifty years of life may not be enough to reach it by the second way. It all depends on how deeply our scalpel cuts through the mind's layers of thought and emotion. This operation, performed so strangely by the mind on the mind with the mind, is yoga.

The gist of this mystical practice is to explore consciousness for its very essence, to delve beneath thoughts for that out of which they are initiated. Nobody ordinarily ever becomes acquainted with mind-in-itself but only with its *workings* in him. For mind is not something which he can picture out in space. Now these ever-restless workings occupy almost the whole of a man's wakeful and dream life. Such an exclusive concentration of attention keeps him from becoming aware of their source. To offset this, we must use a method of self-training which scientifically proposes to divert attention from the particular workings of the mind, which everybody so well knows, to the mind itself, *which hardly anybody knows*. It achieves this by a process of withholding the mental energy and containing it within itself, by the checking of its externalizing movement and the bringing of it into a state of utter stillness.

The fact that we can think about the process of thinking at all shows that we are really superior to, and apart from, it. That which exists in us and enables us to do this is the element out of which all the numerous lines of consciousness arise and into which they merge. Yoga is, in its elementary stage, the isolation of consciousness from physical sensations and, in its advanced stage, the isolation of consciousness from mental thoughts. A little analysis will show that our personality is composed out of its ever-flowing thoughts. They are ever-present with us. Consequently the source out of which they originate, the stuff out of which they are fabricated, must be ever-present too. This is simply the abiding principle of pure Thought. If we can trace our fleeting thoughts back to this abiding principle, it will be the same as tracing out the secret of the holy soul, the Overself, for the two are one and the same.

II

Everything about his subject has been meticulously classified and somewhat drily listed by Patanjali. There are the three kinds of aspirant, the six enhancements of concentration and the five impediments to it, the four stages of yoga, and so on. However it would be a failure in duty not to mention some important points which are not brought out clearly by Patanjali's *Aphorisms,* and which indeed are not brought out in the average yogic circle in India at all, although well understood in the little-known and formerly esoteric school of philosophic yoga.

The first point is that the inhibition of thinking emotion and passion which produces the inward stillness that Patanjali calls "union," is not a final goal but only a background for that goal. When this stillness has been fully attained and expertly mastered, thinking has then to be resuscitated. For the root of that self which really separates man from truth, which blinds him to God and chains him to earth, that self which Jesus asked him to give up if he would find true life, is still there. Its activity is quelled and not annihilated, its self-consciousness lulled and not destroyed. Its last lair must be sought out. The ego itself must be openly confronted until, by a supreme act of insight, it is thoroughly understood in all its depths and ramifications. This insight finally overcomes it and does away with the illusions which it constantly breeds. Orthodox yoga quietens the ego but does not kill its dominance; to achieve this last indispensable task it is needful to go a step beyond yoga. The ego itself is so cunning, its wiles are so clever and tricky that the average yogi is easily deceived into believing it to be subdued when, in fact, it is merely biding its time. Gautama the Buddha had to take this step and tread this ultimate path. He describes how his first teacher, Alara Kamala, was such an adept in yoga that "he would not, sitting on the roadside, be conscious of a caravan of five hundred carts rattling past him." Gautama studied and practiced with Alara Kamala until he became perfect in yoga and reached the same stage as his teacher. He clearly states that he himself fully realized the same goal. Nevertheless he became dissatisfied with it and left Alara Kamala to seek a higher doctrine and a deeper practice.

This should warn us not only that it is not enough to find peace, that we should seek truth also, but that the help of Grace is indispensable in the end. The yogi's will can produce the necessary conditions for bringing about a mystical experience but cannot of itself produce the final consummation of that experience. It must be met by a descent of divine Grace, by a self-revelation from a higher source, if this is to happen.

The second point concerns Patanjali's criticism of mentalism. As this could not be adequately answered without a long discussion rather than a short mention, I shall merely remind the reader once more that, after all, his conclusions are those reached by some schools of yoga only and that there are other schools which advocate mentalism as strongly as he repudiates it.

Thirdly, the yogic self-absorbed contemplation in which all this discipline and training culminates is not the ultimate goal at all. It is only a stage on the way to that goal, which is, to be able to live in the world, not deserting it, while living in the soul at the same time; to be fully alert efficient and conscious while discharging all worthy duties and tasks, yet keeping the innermost part of the mind anchored in the divine stillness which transcends the world.

Fourthly, nor should impoverishment of personal life and indifference to personal development be regarded as the goal. The anti-intellectual, the anti-artistic and the anti-practical attitudes which are so commonly found in the circles of yogis, are merely temporary means to an end and do not constitute permanent ends in themselves. Provided the seeker guards against the dangers of being side-tracked by the conceits of intellect or deceived by the fascinations of art, that is, provided he learns to keep his balance, he will find that the very contrary—the enrichment and development of his individuality are required from him by evolution and by Nature. For instance, whenever mysticism develops on a solely religious foundation, it needs to add the psychological foundation later. Thus balance is preserved. When it develops on a psychological one only, it needs to add the religious to secure the same balance.

The last two points indicate a need of the caution and discrimination with which Westerners should receive any attempt to implant yoga in their midst. We should use it as a help to inspire life, not in the denial of life. We should not throw off the spell of Occidentalism's spiritual superiority complex only to pick up its Oriental analogue. Those who seek truth should not make the mistake of limiting its stretch to a particular hemispheral mind or locating its presence in a particular hemispheral type. They should not, because they have become convinced that there is something to be learnt from the East, cease from a realistic appraisal of the state of things there. They should not, for example, indulge in a superficial condemnation of everything Western and chant an equally superficial paean of praise for everything Eastern. The Very Rev. Dr. Inge points out that Western civilization is very sick but the doctors disagree. "The Indians," he says, "lookers-on, who see most of the game, have their own opinion. They tell us that there are two paths—the path of wisdom and the path of pursuit. The West has chosen the latter. It confounds civilization with comfort and progress, with multiplication of wants, and has made nobody any the happier." But such Indians are not correct in implying that the East alone has chosen the right path and we the path of foolishness. The present day East, like the present day West, does not offer an ideal example. It is an error to ascribe to the East qualities and virtues, knowledge and power which properly belong to no race but to all races. The fact is wisdom is not the exclusive possession of any one people or country. It has been found in the past by individuals scattered everywhere and may be so found again.

The real need is for a new form, not one which shall imitate unsuited past forms or limited hemispheral ones. It should be a twentieth century and global one, wedding mysticism to practicality. An Orient which was mentally and physically incompetent to deal scientifically with the external environment of man is now feeling the results of this deficiency. An Occident which despised meditation, ascetic self-discipline and metaphysical values, is now feeling the painful consequences of this profound lack in its life. We must experiment creatively until we find a composite culture that suits us. The Orient and the Occident are not mutually exclusive in these days of universal inter-communication. The culture of man cannot be modern and complete until it combines the knowledge which has resulted from the labors of the West with that which has resulted from the labors of the East. Both contributions must be put into a common basket. We can profitably use the research-results of the brown men, as we have used those of the white men, and this need not make us any less Western in our standpoint than before. We can still remain loyal to the heritage and the circumstances which are peculiarly our own, even though we take advantage of the knowledge and the discoveries of those who inhabit the lands of the rising sun and add them to our own. We must free ourselves from such narrowing bias as is supplied by the accident of birth or the preference of temperament.

I came home a couple of years ago from several years' work and travel in the Orient convinced that humanity's sickness was global. Since my return, the observations made during journeys in postwar America and Europe have completed this diagnosis and confirmed it. Whatever remedy will have to be found to cure this sickness, our need meanwhile of emotional repose, mind control and inner peace is more than ever before, not only for the personal benefits they give but just as much for the public capacity to judge calmly and rightly the momentous issues confronting us. The future is dark. Millions of people are being converted to a teaching, or forced to walk unwillingly under a banner, which denies the existence of God and denounces the temples of religion, which propagates hatred, practices robbery and spreads violence. We need all the inner strength we can gather to meet this error and terror of our age. We should therefore not let cultural ignorance or racial unfamiliarity prevent us drawing on whatever the Orient can contribute to that strength. We are in such sore plight today that no chance to enlarge our inner resources should be missed, no legitimate way of finding inner relief should be rejected. We need hope and help, not from one quarter alone but from all quarters; therefore we should accept, not only the stimulations of faith which religion brings us but also the stimulations of will and mind which yoga proffers us. The first yoga text as such ever written down was the one which Professor Wood has here so successfully translated. Certain it is that the successful practice of yoga would free us from these obsessions by fear and rid us of these visitations by anxiety. We, poor mortals, who are in Wordsworth's lines:

> "Rolled round in earth's diurnal course
> With rocks, and stones, and trees,"

may not be able to stop the calamities which personal destiny or national history thrust upon us, but if we have been self-trained in yoga we can certainly control favorably our mental attitude and emotional reaction to such calamities. Those who seek relief from contemporary anxieties can find it therein, and those who seek a refuge from contemporary perils can find it there too. However, because both relief and refuge are at first entirely inward and mental, society tends to undervalue them, to regard them as vague dreams of little worth. This is society's great mistake.

If Patanjali's aphorisms have any message at all to the Western world today, it is a message of the need of meditation. This need arises because the need of a personal and inward experience of illumination arises. Historicity and tradition in religion are, we find today, not quite enough. They may lead to lifelessness. Indeed one man who seemed to me to understand Jesus best was not born a Christian at all. He was born a Hindu. In the Maharishee of Arunachala I found the authentic and admirable example in the flesh of what yoga means. More than nine years have passed since I last met him, yet his memory keeps ever-fresh with appreciation and reverence in my heart.

There have always been persons who are attracted towards meditation or who are willing to try it. There are others, especially among creative artists, who practice it quite unconsciously at times; still others who follow it unwittingly by the innate trend of their temperament. Yet meditation is not easy. It involves reaching right down into the very roots of consciousness. This is hard, as those who have tried it can testify, as hard as trying to climb the slippery slopes of a precipitous mountain. Indeed, the ancient Sanskrit texts say that the chances of full success are only with the man whose patience in persevering with the exercises is unwearied and whose efforts are inspired and helped by a competent teacher. The impulses of the personal will have to be conquered. The struggles against personal desire have to be fought. But the gains are great—a true well-being, the doing-away with all the little wars and large divisions within oneself, an end to the agony of being torn from different sides at once. But even if anyone falls short of this, there are lesser rewards on the way. Enchanted hours, which take the sorry bitterness and heavy care out of life, will be thrown to him. Its difficulty should not deter us from trying to learn something of it, for no effort in this direction will be wasted. What we need is the resolution to find a little time for it, the willingness to make a little place for it in our everyday life.

Even if yoga is too unfamiliar and too hard to become popular, that does not really matter. What matters is that our face should be Godward-turned in some way or other, that we should not forget the higher power behind all our lives. There are different ways of approach to this power and each person has to find the way that suits him. The way of yoga attracts a certain type, but it does not attract other types. For them, the simplicity of prayer or the discipline of a good life may perhaps be enough. Let them follow their own road, for it will lead them in the same direction as yoga; that is, it will bring them closer to the holy source of their being. Indeed, there is a point where prayer as communion with the divine or as the adoration of it, is sometimes so overcome by its own feelings as to fall into a state of rapt absorption hardly distinguishable from the yogic state.

This call to religion, this attraction to mysticism, this interest in philosophy comes, if traced to its source, from one and the same place—from the higher part of our being. It is in the state of deep tranquil reverie upon it that the mind receives its loftiest revelations and the heart its holiest suffusions.

The Overself waits with everlasting patience for each man to find it anew. This is the mysterious and glorious secret of human existence, this is the sublime guarantee of human redemption.

Paul Brunton

Practical Yoga

ANCIENT AND MODERN

CHAPTER 1

INTRODUCTORY—AUTHOR
TO READER

This book is the result of over forty-five years of "living with Yoga." With a view to studying this subject in its traditional form, I started to learn the Sanskrit language all those years ago. Before that, I studied the subject as far as it was available in English. I left England and made my home in India when the present century was very young, and there mingled with people interested in yoga. In 1947 I entered the United States on a residential visa, and I am now promoting the subject of yoga here, knowing that it is as well adapted to modern life as to the simpler living of ancient India, and believing that it can make the individual stronger and freer and help to promote social harmony and material progress. It can bring more power into every activity of life, and at the same time purity and peace.

I have felt that these personal remarks are necessary to give the reader confidence in my new translation of the famous Yoga Aphorisms of Patanjali, and in my ability to explain them. I have not wished to trouble the reader with Sanskrit words, as they are quite unnecessary for the practice of yoga. Sanskrit scholars familiar with the use of the language in philosophical works may test for themselves the accuracy of my translation. They will find that it is not a "free" translation, but that it follows very closely the words of the original.

There are, however, a few words from Sanskrit which have been used to such an extent in books in English that they may by now be regarded as adopted into the language. First among these is the word yoga itself; next the word yogī, which means one who practices yoga; and thirdly the word karma, of which the meaning will become very clear in the course of the book.

In our modern culture we have derived benefit from several streams of ancient thought. We have adopted what was essentially good in them and adapted it to the living present. In the main, two streams of such thought have blended in us. Social science and philosophic thought from Greece provided one stream of influence, touching especially our thinking. The religion of the Jews, culminating in the ethical insight and mystical devotion of Jesus, provided another stream of influence, touching our emotions and motives. The isolation of the Hindus kept us much longer from a third stream of ancient culture, coming from a people who had specialized for tens of centuries in human psychology and practical philosophy. That has come into America now, however, in great power—in such a flood that scarcely anyone misses some of its effect, indirect if not direct. It began in this country with Emerson, who helped greatly in the development of the American outlook and the American way of life, an ideology which permeated the schools and gradually produced that social temper of the individual which is the best insurance of the future welfare of the race. Emerson acknowledged the inspiration he derived from Hindu thought. It is related that on a certain occasion a party of young men came to the philosopher and desired to know how they might become learned. He told them to read good books for five hours every day. They asked, "What books?" His answer was, "Any good books that you like." But as they were about to depart he called them back and said, "But do not forget to read the Hindu books." It is said also that in his latter years he always carried a pocket edition of the *Bhagavad Gītā* about with him.

The famous scholar, Professor Max Müller, wrote some

very significant words on this matter, in his book *India: What Can It Teach Us?*, as follows:

"If I were to look over the whole world to find out the country most richly endowed with all the wealth, power and beauty that nature can bestow—in some parts a very paradise on earth—I should point to India. If I were asked under what sky the human mind has most fully developed some of its choicest gifts, has most deeply pondered on the greatest problems of life, and has found solutions of some of them which well deserve the attention even of those who have studied Plato and Kant—I should point to India. And if I were to ask myself from what literature we, here in Europe, we who have been nurtured almost exclusively on the thoughts of Greeks and Romans, and of one Semitic Race, the Jewish, may draw that corrective which is most wanted in order to make our inner life more perfect, more comprehensive, more universal, in fact more truly human, a life, not for this life only, but a transfigured and eternal life—again I should point to India."

I am not proposing that we should Indianize ourselves, but that we should welcome, adopt, adapt, and make use of a system of thought and psychological practice which we are bound to recognize as effective, do we but study it. The old Yoga Aphorisms of Patanjali are for use here and now chiefly as a focusing point of our thought and purpose. Beginning with that, we can select, employ and adapt what suits us, and find in it an addition to our present living, a poised vitality, a clarity and inflexibility of purpose and an intelligent use of our mind-machine which will profit both individual and society.

Patanjali is generally believed by Hindu scholars to have lived and arranged his Yoga Aphorisms about 300 B.C. Some place him later, but the date does not matter. He divides them into four sections: I, On Contemplation; II, On Yoga in Daily

Life; III, On Psychic Powers; and IV, On Independence. In this book I have grouped the aphorisms according to the natural course of study and practice, instead of giving the most advanced and difficult part near the beginning, as Patanjali does. Patanjali was very largely catering for the born yogīs, those fortunate people who love yoga and proceed into its most advanced practices without noticing any difficulty at all. Only in his Second Section does he begin to offer modes of practice for the ordinary beginner in yoga. I have ventured to put the course in the order which I have found by long experience to be most helpful to the Western student. I have, however, given the entire translation in Patanjali's order in an appendix, and have also planned this as an index, so that each aphorism can easily be found in the main part of the book.

Those who approach the subject of yoga do so from three quite different points of view. One group says: "We want to make our lives richer and stronger in the immediate future. We do not seek something different from the kind of life we now know, but we want it much improved, both inside and outside, that is to say, in mind and body, and in environment. We want clear, strong minds, well stocked with knowledge about the art of living, and we want tasty and wholesome food; sensible, clean and good clothing; well-equipped houses, with comfort, sanitation, security and beauty; happy families; good and friendly neighbors; and community benefits such as good schools and libraries, honest newspapers, swimming pools and roads. We are not averse to regular work and even labor, but we want ample leisure with good entertainment by magazines, radio, music, the theater, public lectures and forums, good transport and access to holiday places in the mountains and at the seaside. We do not seek the solution of the mysteries of life—what the world really is or what we ourselves really are—but we want a stronger, richer life. Can yoga help us to that?"

The answer is that it can, for it says to the inquirer: "Your success depends upon how you work in the world. It needs that you look every fact that concerns you straight in the eye and know it for what it is to the senses, and then deal with it with all the knowledge you have and with decision. It needs that you ponder your own thoughts and feelings until you know what you want, without groping about, without a miserable acceptance of negative satisfaction, and without resignation. It needs that you meet your neighbors with the clear-sighted knowledge that, taken as a whole, they are all very similar to yourself, and the complete abandonment of superiority and inferiority complexes. It needs that you govern your appetites at the same time that you enjoy and satisfy them. It needs, above all, clarity of mental imagery and mental vision, to which the practice of yoga directly leads."

The second group says: "Our vision soars beyond that. We want psychic faculties and powers. We want clairvoyance, clairaudience, psychometry. We want to dissolve things and to create them by thought, without hands. We want to travel in astral bodies, and mental bodies and buddhic bodies, and to converse with the dead. We want life as it is known on earth with the senses enhanced, but without difficulties and restrictions, and with vastly greater greatness, and more color and light and swelling chords of heavenly harmony."

"All right," says the yoga school. "You can have almost all of that—short of converse with the dead."

The third group says: "We want to solve the mystery of life. We look at ourselves and say, 'What strange things we are!' We look at our lives, and ask, 'To what end are all these pains and pleasures, and these pleasures of pain and pains of pleasure?' We want to understand, to know the truth about life and things with some new knowing, better than the wooden kind of knowledge that looks at things and gives them names."

The yoga school says, "Good. You have come to the right

place. We tell you that the human mind is not the instrument for the knowledge you seek; but we tell you, too, that the same mind, when purified and cleansed, like a mirror without dust, can reflect the Truth you need and stand you at its very threshold. We tell you that it is not the mindless creatures who are nearest to that vision, but those whose minds are clean and clear and pure. The pure in heart shall see." Yes, yoga is a well-thought-out means to the fulfillment of mind-life in something beyond it.

The yoga school is realistic, mystical and scientific—realistic in that it insists upon the actual existence of the external world and a normal valuation of sense-perceptions; mystical in that its aim is to bring its students to a truth beyond the mind; and scientific in that its methods of mental practice and training embody the best of psychological knowledge. I recommend it in the spirit of the old words familiar to us all: "Finally, brethren, whatsoever things are true, whatsoever things are honest, whatsoever things are just, whatsoever things are pure, whatsoever things are lovely, whatsoever things are of good report; if there be any virtue, and if there be any praise, think on these things." [1]

[1] Ph. 4, 8.

CHAPTER 2

THE FIVE IDEAS AND
THEIR CONTROL

Patanjali opens his subject with a statement that his book is to be an instructional treatise of yoga:

I, 1. "Now, instruction in yoga."

Exactitude was a characteristic of the old Hindu philosophers, and here we have it. Patanjali does not say "an account of yoga," for the simple reason that yoga can only be known by experience resulting from practice. Instruction there can be in the practice of yoga, and reasons can be given for the various instructions, and psychological principles can be enunciated in connection with those reasons—but yoga is to be known in the living of it and cannot be described like an object in the street. The practice of yoga in India goes back into ancient times. Patanjali does not propound something new; he simply proposes to give instruction, and he is acclaimed by all a most competent teacher of this art.

The dictionaries tell us that yoga means primarily union, junction, connection. Its goal is the attainment of unity—but that is to be realized in experience, not to be mentally defined. This much we may say, however, about union, that it is in some way the perfection of that unity which appears as essential to the success of mental, bodily and ethical life. Union would be the fulfillment of our most essential human urges.

In science our touchstone is unity, inasmuch as we try to know things in relation to one another, and through their relations to know better and better their properties and functions. We strive to understand their enveloping and ultimately all-embracing laws, in brief, their unity. In religion, with its departments of ethics and devotion, again we find the same urge—an ethic to unify all living things and a devotion to one divine life and rule. In art, we find our progressive satisfaction in the production of harmony that unifies what is grouped within it—whether in a piece of sculpture, painting, music or poetry. And even that modern phase of art which seems at first to present a jumble of unrelated things derives its merit from the ability of its votaries to see in it a deeper truth. In philosophy there is a constant seeking of those laws which show the fitting of life to environment. Even in ordinary living, where men and women propose no great or distant aims, there is real pleasure in their well-planned homes, where the eye is delighted with cleanliness (dirt is matter in the wrong place, a violation of unity) and a pleasing grouping of colors and forms, ministering to rest and restful activity and to nourishment and the unities of health.

The word yoga comes from a verbal root which means to unite, or join or combine. The same root also appears as meaning to meditate, but we may infer that somewhere in the past the latter root meaning has been derived from the former, as the ancient practice of meditation was used as the principal means to the fulfillment of the urge to unity.

I have to put in a safeguarding statement here. People sometimes ask: "Unity with what?" and try to answer the question tentatively: "Perhaps it is with the divine life, or with the one life, or with the true self, or with the eternal, or with the infinite." But in yoga we must not try to predetermine the goal or the issue of our lives and works. There is no "with" in this matter. We must—this is imperative—be content that unity shall reveal itself to us in its own way when we have removed the obstacles to the unity which are within our own lives, without, however, losing the zest of life. That central urge in us which we feel as zest is in some way a part of the unity, and its joy is a promise of its and our ultimate fulfillment.

Yoga means not only the unity; it has come to mean also the efforts and practices helpful towards that fulfillment, and useful for the thinning and removal of all coverings of the light. In his second aphorism Patanjali plunges us headlong into the task:

I, 2. "*Yoga is the control of the ideas in the mind.*"

With equal boldness and clarity the teacher next tells us what happens when all these ideas in the mind are controlled and when they are not controlled. He says:

I, 3. "*Then there is the dwelling of the Looker in his own proper nature.*"
I, 4. "*Otherwise there is identification with the ideas.*"

This is not the point at which to enlarge upon the nature of that being which is at the core of our being, and his relation to the mind and the ideas in the mind. These discussions will come up in their proper places further on in our study. Here Patanjali only invites us to consider the present situation—we are not truly ourselves because we are not being ourselves, but have surrendered ourselves to circumstances. These circumstances are not merely the facts of life and the world, but also and even more the ideas in our minds.

We must here note one psychological principle in passing— for our liberation from this bondage and the realization of our true state of being it is sufficient to control the ideas. It is not necessary to control the facts. Here Patanjali takes it for granted that ideas in the mind govern all the facts that have to do with our bondage, for ideas rule the world, and forms or facts flow in obedience to them. He proceeds on the assumption that, just as we make our tables and chairs and streets and towns and bridges and cultivated fields according to the ideas in our minds, with the bodily organs acting merely as obedient tools, so do we make the whole of our environment; "we" here being collective—we do a lot of this work together and enjoy the proceeds both directly and by exchange.

While we are involved in these ideas we are in bondage. To obtain release, we must control them. Patanjali will tell us how to do this, and in what direction to guide them—for control does not mean suppression, but guidance.

The teacher next asks us to observe what these forms in the mind, called ideas, are.

I, 5. "The ideas are of five kinds, painful and pleasant."

The five kinds will be described in aphorisms I, 6 to I, 11.

In Patanjali's school of thought all objects in the world are regarded as intensely real. Ideas in the mind share that objective quality, so an idea is not a mere evanescent bubble in a flow of thought, but something very definite and durable. The mind is something like a home, in and about which there are pleasant and painful things. You may be sitting writing in your library and not thinking at all about the lovely front lawn with its two or three companionable trees and its beds of flowers, but they are there and you are not wholly unconscious of them.

Similarly, in the mind we have a great number and variety of idea-things which, having once been admitted and established there, even though forgotten and unseen at any particular time, remain there and are not without their pleasurable and painful influence at all times. Yoga requires us to deal positively with these things of the mind, just as we do with those in our homes. "These old chairs must go; we will have a new davenport instead," says the lady of the house. She will not leave them there to molder away.

A forgotten painful experience in connection with which the mind establishes a strong idea is forgotten in course of time, but it still casts its somber shadow over present pleasures and makes them less colorful than they would otherwise be, acting like an unseen abscess at the root of a bad tooth. As to the "aching tooth" ideas, most people know them well, in the form of worry.

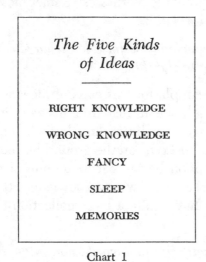

The Five Kinds of Ideas

RIGHT KNOWLEDGE

WRONG KNOWLEDGE

FANCY

SLEEP

MEMORIES

Chart 1

In practical life the pleasantness or unpleasantness of a thing is often a matter of degree. The temperature of the bath water may be pleasant, but the bath may become painful by the addition of either hot or cold water. Pleasures intensified turn to pain. What we are to understand here is that the practice of control will apply to both pleasant and painful ideas, and to all the five kinds now to be enumerated:

I, 6. "Right knowledge, wrong knowledge, fancy, sleep and memories."

Patanjali goes on to define the five:

I, 7. "Right knowledges are perceptions, inferences and testimonies."

These are the three ways of obtaining correct ideas. Some are received into the mind as perceptions (as when we see

a tree and know it), some as inferences (as when we assume
that our friend Mr. Jones has a brain. "All men have brains;
Mr. Jones is a man; therefore Mr. Jones has a brain"), some as
testimonies by reliable witnesses. Sometimes testim is
called verbal information.

*I, 8. "Wrong knowledge is false knowledge, fixed in a form
not according to the thing."*

A standard example for this class of ideas is as foll
farmer is coming home at dusk from his work in the fields.
the distance he sees a man standing, but when he gets near
finds it is only a post. Or, on the ground he sees a snake, but
on closer perception he finds it to be only a piece of rope.
"Man" and "snake" were wrong knowledge. It is considered
that most of us have quite a large collection of such wrong
ideas.

*I, 9. "Fancy is settling upon word-knowledge, there being no
such thing."*

An example of this class of ideas is, "The horns of a rabbit."
Much of *Alice in Wonderland* and *A Midsummer Night's
Dream* would come under this class. I may mention that and
anjali does not condemn such fancies. In yoga we are not primarily concerned in obtaining right knowledge and destroying or correcting wrong knowledge and fancies about th
in the world. The aim is to control all classes of ideas.

*I, 10. "Sleep is the idea based upon the conception of ab-
sence."*

In this philosophy, sleep is not regarded as a total cessation
of the mind's activity. There is still an idea there. The mind
dwells upon the idea of the absence of everything; so this idea
needs a class to itself. It is not considered to be an unconscious state. That is why, it is argued, when we wake in the
morning we may say: "I slept well," meaning not that we now

feel refreshed and we therefrom infer that we slept well, but that we remember that we slept well, that we enjoyed the pleasurable idea of absence of anything. We may note here that the mere suppression of ideas—not the system of control propounded in the aphorisms—would be only the concentration of the mind on absence, which would not lead to yoga.

"*Memory is the non-loss of objects in knowledge.*"

Long ago the Hindu philosophers posed the question: Does memory re-present only the act of knowing the object, or does it remember the object? They generally held that memory re-presents the experience of the occasion when the object was present; so the answer is, both. Along with this there is, of course, the knowledge that this is a re-presentation of past experience, but this knowledge is present knowledge, separate from memory.

We have reviewed all the five classes or groupings of forms in the mind. There can now be no doubt that these are what we today call ideas, and that they are of the nature of mental furniture. If a man closes his eyes and looks into his own mind he will find it furnished with various ideas, just as when he opens his eyes again he will find that his house is furnished. He calls his mental furniture knowledge, and, if asked, will say that he has a lot of knowledge of things connected with his business, his daily life, his friends and associates, and his favorite reading. If questioned further as to whether he knows the names of the streets in Paris or London or Istambul, he will answer that he does not, and furthermore he does not want to know them and does not need to know them. So, then, ideas, like house furniture, are for use.

Ideas are material for thinking with. Generally, however, what happens is not thinking but mental drift. I look at my fountain pen. At once it becomes a starting point for mental drift. I remember that it was a presentation, that it gave me trouble by leaking when it was new, and that I took it for

repair to the shop in Bangalore where it was bought. Banga-
lore—lovely, sunny town. Years ago I was president of a college in the same area, affiliated with the University of Madras.
I made the designs for some of the college buildings. The
workmen quarried the rock locally, hammer-dressed the
stones and laid them by hand in mortar. That was good gran-
ite. It rang like a bell. How fond I was of the rock sections
when I was a student of geology in the Institute of Tech-
nology in Manchester. We were all proud of the college. It
was modeled to some extent on the Boston Tech. I like Boston. I stayed there, or rather in the suburb of Cambridge, for
a week or two in a vacant house. There was a lady who used
to bring groceries in, and she and my wife cooked things and
we ate them, in company with several friends. Her name was
Mrs. Gardner. Yes, she took us to see an Italian garden, which
a relative of hers had transported from Italy to Boston. Italy
—beautiful, sunny Italy—Mussolini gone—a new Italy—
with what future?—a renaissance of art without material ambition? Ambition—I remember what Epictetus thought about
that . . .

And so the drift goes on and on, though not forever, as some
may think. It is an instructive exercise to let it go on an
watch it to the end. This automatically cleanses the mind.

It is not thinking, but drift. It is not control. It is not the
use of ideas. Thinking is the use of ideas. Suppose a student
is asked whether the three angles of any triangle amount together to two right angles and, if so, why. He must hold
steady in his mind the idea of lines, angles and triangles, and
reason about them until he gets the solution. His idea of a
triangle must not drift away to the triangle in an orchestra,
connection with drums—what are those skins made of?—the
slaughter yards—the prairies—cowboys—the dude ranch—
and so on.

Thinking implies control, the temporary stoppage of drift.
In yoga we shall learn that there is such a process as complete

thinking, which is meditation, and that that leads on to contemplation—but enough of that for the present, for it is ideas and their control that we are studying now.

Patanjali has no objection to control by degrees and stages. We may, if we like, control the commonly painful ideas first and live lives resulting from association with pleasant ideas for a long time; but ultimately our essential urge will cause us to tire of these also, to find them boring to painfulness, and so to move on. This aspect of the matter will come up further on.

Supplementary notes to Chapter 2.

(1). Why does Patanjali specifically mention the five classes or kinds of ideas? Because the very first point in control of ideas depends upon our recognizing their class. This is also the basis of mental health. When an idea comes up, do we not instantly classify it, that is, see it as a memory, or a fancy, or a truth, or one of the others? To mistake a fancy for a truth, or a memory, or an error would be a piece of insanity. It reminds me of the kindergarten exercises in which small children are encouraged to put square plates in square holes, round ones in round and so on. So we begin yoga with the perception of the five kinds of ideas. To attempt any maturing of the mind by rational exercises— analogous to physical exercises for the body during youth—without this instinctive classification of ideas would lead only to trouble.

(2). Why does Patanjali specially mention the fact that ideas are painful and pleasant? Because, even the slightest and most casual thought or mental image of anything carries with it some mental pain or pleasure. Sometimes the associations are wrong, as when a gentleman acquired two little dogs, and when he picked up his walking-stick to go for a walk, one little dog capered about with pleasure and the other crouched trembling under the sofa. The import of this knowledge will become clear when we study uncoloredness (*vairāgya*) in Chapter 3.

PRACTICE AND UNCOLOREDNESS

Patanjali proceeds to describe the two general means of achieving control of ideas:

I, 12. "Control of them is by practice and uncoloredness."

The first of these is very easy to understand. The practice of control is not merely, and not even necessarily, regular practice at stated times and intervals. It is, even more, practice at any odd time when you think of it—just observe the drift I have already mentioned and then stop the drift and think instead. It is also aided by the practice of observation. When you have occasion to look at something, or to listen to something, or to taste or feel or smell something, pull yourself together and put yourself, your whole attention, into it, so that the square thing becomes, as it were, more square, and the blue more blue—do not be content with casualness. As to precise methods for formal practice—we shall come to them in due course, in the form of what are called the eight limbs of yoga.

I, 13. "In this matter, practice is the effort towards steadiness."
I. 14. "It becomes firmly grounded when attended to devotedly and without interruption for a long time."

We must just go on quietly doing the thing, not in spasms but more or less frequently, and the sense of effort will pass away. The mood for it will then become habitual and it will become natural. At any stage in the process, it must be remembered, effort means only mental effort, with no bodily strain or abnormality of any kind.

I, 15. "Uncoloredness is the consciousness of power of one who is free from thirst for objects seen or heard about."

To understand this, we must study it in relation to our essential purpose of control of the ideas in the mind. Either we

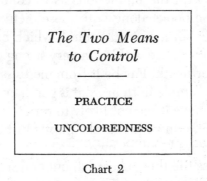

Chart 2

control the ideas, or they control us. In most cases they govern people's lives because the people have strong desires—a thirst for the objects they present to the mind.

Some people have faith in the pictures of heaven described in religious books—and I must say that when I was translating the principal Sanskrit book on this subject, the *Garuda Purāna*, forty years ago, I was charmed by the lovely pictures of broad roads without dust, bordered by shapely trees, with people peacefully walking at the sides, and the unhasty traffic of beautiful carriages and bulls and horses and elephants, while at the roadside there were grassy banks enjoyed by cows, and streams of pure water beautified by groups of pretty ducks, and in the distant view friendly clouds in the blue above and gracious mountains bordering the whole scene, and then, when you came to the town you were to find yourself in a veritable garden city, with peaceful homes and grand and stately public buildings in which common men and women, and philosophers and kings and even the gods themselves foregathered in polite and friendly conversation and the enjoyment of fruits and other edibles suitable to such occasions.

This is one of the "objects heard about," that is, presented in words in the scriptures. People of simple faith may have their whole lives governed by such ideas, and they will live in accordance with the injunctions as to conduct which are presented in the books along with these pictures. Their lives are governed by an idea in the mind, which creates in them a desire to enjoy—more, a thirst, a very strong desire to enjoy —such life after death. Far be it from me to say one word to diminish such a simple faith in what is good, but it is not yoga, and those who have it are not likely to turn to yoga for a long time. It is essential in yoga that the pupil must take to it absolutely from an impulse of his own.

In other cases the things heard about and seen and desired are not in the distant view. The young people have married and they want a pretty home and a garden plot, and the touch of the hands of children. Some people want scenes and objects of excitement and violence, and the satisfaction of the desire for possessions and great fame and power, and even the enjoyment of injury and cruelty.

These are all colored by ideas, governed by ideas. Their driving power is not within themselves. It is only thirst for things that they have, not knowledge of the greatest good. They are ruled by pleasure, and sometimes by pain and the fear of pain. This habit of pleasure causes the coloredness. It is as though a block of glass were placed on a sheet of green paper and thus permeated by the green light, then on red, and on blue. Thirst for things leads to coloredness, which the yogī regards as servitude and bondage. In his path of life he prescribes uncoloredness.

Let us see how this affects the practice of meditation which the yogī puts before himself. He meditates perhaps upon a rose; in the perfection of his meditation he means to go right through the rose into contemplation of the reality with which the visible object is only partially tinged. The objective rose is objectively only matter, energy and natural law, but to even the slightest contemplation it is a window into some reality which is not in the matter, energy and law. But if, in his meditation on the rose, he is to be assailed by a desire for a little cake, or something stronger, or by fears (which are negative desires) of tomorrow's weather or stock market, or by anger-pictures of someone who has been insulting to him, his meditation is doomed. He must have uncoloredness, if his meditation is to succeed.

Have I drawn a picture of a man who does not take delight in anything, and is without repugnance even for a cesspool? I hope not. Our yogī is not to be a dead man; on the contrary, he has to be the most alive of men. He has, by his concentration, to find that things flame more brightly for him than they did before, which means that he is more alive and receptive to reality. But he is not to be ruled from the outside; he is to be master in his own mind and the operator and governor of his ideas.

The fact is, our yogī must be a philosopher. A philosopher is a man who knows what things do to him, and what he can do to them and with them; and he values ideas and experiences for use. In the yoga schools we posit a real man or self at the core of our being. This self is not produced or made by any other thing; also it is not a producer of anything. We must not say that it thinks, or loves or wills or does anything—for the simple reason that if we do so we shall be putting it in the category of ideas, and will again become governed by an idea in the mind.

When we think of ourselves we put ourselves in the category of ideas, and a yoga-practice based on that would result in our finding ourselves back again at the old stand with just another idea. But we find that we have a faculty with which to govern ideas—something we call the will. I will venture to affirm that with thought we perceive things and ideas, with love-perception or feeling we become aware of other people's lives, and with will-perception we receive at least a little intuition of the incorruptible self. That is reflected in us and appears then as the will aspect of the mind, which governs ideas and guides them towards their fulfillment in the revelation of unity. Of that high and last point of yoga at which the will is poised for its final flight, nothing can possibly be described in terms of outward experience.

It is enough for us to know that on the path of yoga we ally ourselves with the positive principle in us, which governs forms. To do so requires that we have the uncoloredness which is so emphatically prescribed. We shall then find that in the fulfillment of our thinking we intuit truth, goodness and beauty, which are all defined by unity.

The yogī lives on the wing, not in a cage. Blake caught the idea and put it into a verse:

> "He who takes to himself a joy
>   Doth the wingéd life destroy,
> But he who kisses the joy as it flies
>   Lives in eternity's sunrise."

The yogī lives and acts like everybody else, but his interest lies in the unities. If, being a man, he sees a beautiful woman, he may enjoy that fully, but he will not desire to hold and possess. If a woman, in a modern land like America, the yoginī (feminine of yogī) will probably dress and color herself as women do now, for beauty in her own world (will working towards unity), for pleasure of others (love living unity), and for the ordering of things (thought planning unity).

May I here say something about the psychology of unity, to show that its simplicity implies not paucity but harmony, and that it is not inconsistent with variety and even complexity? A pen in the hand in the act of writing is a simple idea, because it is harmonious, but a pen dancing a jig on horseback would be an idea difficult to hold, because incongruous, and its various elements would soon spring apart on the removal of our restraining will. Will, love and thought all make for simplicity, casting their unity over things, persons and ideas. Our yoginī will probably see that all garments, from hat to shoes, form one picture, not several, and that the body inside the clothes is as perfect as it can be made.

Patanjali goes on:

I, 16. "It is higher when there is no thirst for the Qualities of Nature, on account of knowledge about the real man."

I have referred here to knowledge *about* the real man or self, not to knowledge *of* that, as such a leap into infinity would be inconsistent with the practice of yoga, and only consistent with the final attainment or fulfillment of yoga. But we have some knowledge about the real man or self quite early, and that helps to take our uncoloredness not only beyond the danger of common ideas and things, but beyond anything conceivable in the realms of matter, energy and law, which are the three principles or Qualities of Nature, or the external or objective world.

It is considered in old Hindu science and philosophy that these three principles or fundamentals are the ultimates out of which all objective forms are made by compounding in different proportions. They go far behind the Western conceptions of atoms or even electrons, and yet every Western scientist acknowledges their sway.

The same set of three qualities is used to describe the prominent qualities of anything in Nature, as it is considered that in the compounding of forms they occur in different proportion. In their widest connotations they are matter, energy and natural law. As qualities in particular things, words such as the following are often used to describe them: (*a*) materiality, resistivity, inertia, dullness, darkness; (b) motion, activity, restlessness; and (c) law, order, rhythm, harmony, purity.

In the present connection the meaning is clear. The yogī is not to be caught in any of the material "isms." He will not feel himself based in or supported by or dependent on matter, nor as a power house of energy and dynamic life, nor as belonging to some sweet, harmonizing and all-embracing law or controlling principle. No, for at last he must not be colored by any of these. Something still better is in store for him. I am reminded of the old statement, "Eye hath not seen, nor ear heard, neither hath entered into the heart of man, the things which God hath prepared for them that love him." [1]

[1] I Cor. 2, 9.

Supplementary note to Chapter 3.

Where I have used the word "uncoloredness," some have spoken of detachment, desirelessness, indifference, dispassion etc. The word is *vairāgya*. My translation is, I think, quite perfect, for *rāga* means color or dye. We have to acquire the mature use of our own mind-powers in relation to things and events, so that our lives are not colored by our old pleasure and pain reactions. As it is, our minds only too often react without consulting us.

Desire (*rāga*) is defined by Patanjali as a consequence of pleasure (see p. 72), which indicates its character. Any implication of general dislike (*dwesha*) for the world and retreat from it on this ground would be wrong.

CHAPTER 4

YOGA IN DAILY LIFE

It frequently happens that when a man has made up his mind to practice yoga seriously, he begins to think that to do it successfully he must go to India. But this world is all of a piece, and America is just as good as India for this purpose. Then he says he must find some place of great quiet and retirement in America, if not in India. Again I say he is wrong. It is, in fact, not unusual for a teacher of yoga in India to send a would-be pupil into the world of ordinary life for several years, with instructions to practice a certain portion of the yoga course and then return to him for further consideration of the matter.

This is that portion of the yoga course which is to be carried on in the midst of active ordinary life. It is real yoga, not merely a preparation for it, but it is the stage of the novice.

We may speak of three stages. The first is that of the person who merely takes an interest in yoga. He feels that he would like to understand what it means, because he is not satisfied with life as it is. He is called "desirous of rising." The second stage is that of the person who has commenced deliberate and fairly regular practice. He is the "novice." The third is the stage of the yogī who is becoming expert in the use of meditation and contemplation. He has "risen to yoga" or is "mounted on yoga."

This yoga in active life is practiced in India by hundreds of thousands of family men during the day, along with some study and meditation in their spare time. For example, in the cities many professional men, merchants and office workers rise at perhaps 6 A.M., take a little exercise followed by a wash

45

all over, then read some portion of scripture or philosophy and practice meditation until about 8, after which they take their morning meal, and arrive at their office ready for the day's work by about 9 to 10 o'clock. This unhurried "novitiate" gradually and insensibly leads on to full competence in the arts of meditation and contemplation. While at office and doing their business, they attend also to the practices of daily life which are enjoined in the course I am about to describe.

This is also generally the course for the novice who has presented himself before a guru, or teacher, and has been told to go back into ordinary life and practice the triple daily-life yoga for a period of years. And this is exactly what the average Western man or woman who wants to take up the practice of yoga should do, for you cannot plunge headlong into yoga.

Let the novice not promise anything to himself, but let him proceed with the work. He is not called upon to prejudge the future, either what will happen, or what he will at some future time decide to do. Nor is he to judge himself in the light of success or failure. The novice does not know what success and failure in yoga are. Inasmuch as yoga is an adventure into an unknown field for him, any decision on his part to "attain" a definite goal can only anchor him to something which may really be only an object by the wayside. I wish to guard the novice against the two dangers of self-judgment and the fixing of goals, and to tell him that as he is calling into expression high forces within and behind and above his present level of self he must let them do their work in him.

Patanjali begins this course with the statement:

II. 1. "Yoga in active life consists of Body-conditioning, Self-study and Attentiveness to God.

These are the three things to be practiced in everyday life, as yoga in the midst of action. They are definitely prescribed for the man who cannot immediately rise to the successful achievement of complete contemplation and insight, that is, for him who cannot at once fully control all the contents of his outward-turned mind. There are certain instincts in the mind of every man which make him a slave to his own ideas. Ideas rule him, whereas he should rule and use them, the proper condition of his mind being that of a power among ideas, which looks at them, takes hold of them, sorts, classifies, ar-

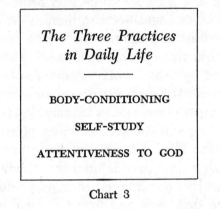

**The Three Practices
in Daily Life**

—

BODY-CONDITIONING

SELF-STUDY

ATTENTIVENESS TO GOD

Chart 3

ranges and combines them, or, in brief, treats them in the mind just as we treat furniture in our dwellings or machinery in our factories. Perhaps this simile does not go far enough, for these ideas have a quasi life of their own. They are a bit like pet animals as well as furniture.

I say quasi life, because they draw their vitality from the man himself. There are certain instincts of his (which we will study in Chapter 5) through which he feeds them, to such an extent that they sometimes positively prey upon his vitals. He must understand these and so become their gentle master, before he can have true peace of mind, which is the same as freedom.

It was said in the blood-curdling old stories about vampires that when a man was attacked by one of these, which sucked his blood in the night, he was infected by it so that he himself became a vampire in course of time. That will do as an allegory for the condition of the average man. If he is a slave to his possessions, still more is he a slave to his ideas. And the only way to weaken that slavery and prepare the way for the powers of meditation and contemplation is to practice the three divisions of the yoga of daily life.

1. *Body-conditioning*. The verbal root from which the technical word for this practice is derived means "to heat." Applied to daily life, it means to be very *ardent* in the bodily training leading to yoga. Because there is an implication of considerable effort and firmness of will in carrying out this part of the work, many people have thought of it as meaning self-denial and hardship. This practice is often thus incorrectly associated with painful austerity or even mortification.

When one visits certain steps leading down to the waters of the river Ganges at Benares, one may often see men who have carried the idea of control of body to such unintelligent lengths that they have injured their bodies. Some have blinded themselves or rendered themselves dumb by deliberate injury to their eyes and tongues; some have rendered an arm lifeless by holding it stiffly aloft until it has withered —a long list of these mortifications could be given. Such excesses indicate a measure of insanity. (In India the insane are not put in institutions, unless dangerous, and "the village idiot" is a common sight.) These men obviously miss the real intention of this practice, which means not to mortify the flesh with torture or the soul with pain, but to cleanse the body inside and out, and bring it to such a condition of healthy functioning that it will present the minimum of obstruction to the more advanced practices of yoga.

To put the matter briefly, it means to do for the body what you believe to be best to bring it into perfect condition—what you would call perfect physical condition in a dog or a horse if you were preparing to take it to a show. If you believe, for example, that it is not good to sprinkle salt on your food, this practice requires that you will act accordingly. You may like the taste of excess salt, but the will steps in firmly and says, "No." I say "if you believe"; all the virtue lies in that "if," for Body-conditioning may in one person require abstention from salt and in another person the definite use of much salt, according to their beliefs. This principle applies to everything —food, clothing, exercise, rest, talking, study, work and all.

Let no one imagine that in this matter the senses are being flouted; on the contrary, one who wishes to go to the length of abstention from salt beyond what naturally comes in normal food will tell you that your loss of the coarse pleasure of the taste of excess salt is more than compensated by the finer pleasure of the real taste of potatoes, or whatever it may be. To take another instance—the quantity of food. If a man finds that he is accumulating too much fat over the abdomen, he should know that there is occasion for control of the quantity or kind of food he is taking, or for some form of exercise.

This practice is the use of the will for the good of the body. It will succeed when there is a definite decision not to allow the appetites to take charge of our actions, but to govern them with intelligence, and in all ways to do what we think best for the good condition of the body. It also is the way to the greatest happiness of the body. I knew five brothers who illustrated this point. Two of them became successful and rich men. But they had no self-control. They ate and drank too much, and of the wrong things, and died comparatively young after ten years of bodily misery, lighted up only by the pleasures of taste. The other three brothers lived on into healthy and comfortable old age. If Body-conditioning is rightly done, we shall live at peace with the body, which will enjoy in natural measure the pleasures that accompany and stimulate healthy functioning; and what is more, we shall enjoy that healthy functioning itself, as a good animal does, and in old age we shall quietly decline, until one day we say peaceably to ourselves: "It is enough; I will go now," and will then pass away quietly in our sleep.

Let me not be misunderstood in this matter of healthy living. We do not eat or abstain from eating such and such a thing "in order to be well," nor take exercise "in order to be well." We both eat and abstain for pleasure, but we study where pleasure lies, and see that it does not turn into pain. Yoga prescribes healthy enjoyment of appetites related to functions, but not one inch beyond that functional purpose intelligently understood. "In order to be well" comes in only when by past errors we have created a bad condition of the body in some respect, and it can apply only in some few particulars of our active life—not to our general living. Otherwise, eating is to be an enjoyment, exercise an enjoyment, sleeping and waking an enjoyment and—I hope the reader will understand this—the slow decline into old age (when the "ache of hot youth" has passed) also an enjoyment. We are not whipping a wild animal into sullen obedience. We are living intelligently to the very tips of our fingers and toes.

The average man does not live intelligently, as a man should. With the instincts of an animal and the cunning of a man, he lives. In the state of Nature, love of food drives an animal on. Generally it has to work or hunt all the time to get enough for healthy functioning, but man, clever fellow, has learned to produce ten times his needs, and it comes to his larder often without any effort on his part; and more, when his natural appetite for it has been satisfied and his hunger has gone to sleep, his imagination causes desire for more of the pleasure he remembers. Then he awakens the sleeper with stimulating and exciting condiments added to his food, so as to enjoy more and more of those pleasures of taste. He is a cunning fellow, but he is an almost incredible fool.

On the other hand, the yogī, even the novice in yoga, practices Body-conditioning, which is intelligent bodily living. The living is spontaneous: the intelligence finds the right place and measure for it in the midst of human life. For this reason many of the yogīs of India are misunderstood. If they

want to sing, they sing; if they want to dance, they dance—
anywhere. And the clever fellows, the ordinary men, call
them half-wits.

Another authority—Swātmarāma Swāmī, in *Light on the
Yoga of In and Out Breathing*, a work produced many centuries after Patanjali, wrote: "Yoga does not succeed when
accompanied by excessive eating, exhaustive occupation, too
much talking, adhering to painful vows, promiscuous company and fickleness. It becomes successful by energy, enter-
prise, perseverance, philosophy, resolution and solitude."

After stating that moderate eating means filling the stomach three-quarters full of bland and tasteful foods and drinks,
Swātmarāma Swāmī goes on to describe the foods unsuitable
for a yogī. He says: "Bitter, acid, pungent, salty and hot
foods, myrabolans, betel, jujube fruit, oil, sesamum, mustard,
intoxicants, fish, goat and other meats, curdled milk, butter-
milk, gram, oil-cake, asafoetida and garlic are called unwhole-
some foods." He then says that a yogī should take tasteful and
gratifying food, including milk, pleasing to the senses and
nourishing to the body, and follows this statement with a list
in which he mentions wheat, rice, barley, milk, butter, sugar-
candy, honey, dry ginger, cucumber, various vegetables and
good water. Further, he says that in the beginning a yogī
should avoid bad company, fires, sexual activity, early bathing, fasting and hard work. He adds that success will come
to all who practice—young, old, or very old, and even the ill
and weak—but not to the idle, not by merely talking about
yoga, and not by merely dressing like a yogī.

From this it may be seen how rules and regulations were
brought in by various teachers, whereas Patanjali was all for
the living laws of the inner self, operating through the novice's own will and judgment, and leading to his own decisions.
He lays down no rules of eating etc., but in II, 43, he
says: "From Body-conditioning, with the decline of impurity,
come the powers of the body and the senses."

I have looked at Body-conditioning from the outside of the man. From the inside it implies the functioning and development of the will. The will is that quiet power in us by which we change ourselves, that is, our own feelings, thoughts and body. Observing in ourselves the operations of will, feeling and thought, we find that with thought we know things, and plan to alter or arrange them; with feeling we know and affect other living beings; and with the will we know and govern ourselves.

We are not wholly unconscious of the divine spark in ourselves, and even a little of that knowledge gives us the dignity to maintain our center of life, or will, unsullied and free. The blustering and overbearing attitude to others that some people show is not will. It advertises, in fact, their own susceptibility to such tactics, and thereby indicates their dependence upon external things. But some quiet people can say "I will" with quiet confidence and little by little events fall into line for them and they have real success. I remember always with the greatest pleasure that old Stoic who was confronted by a tyrant who said to him, "Do you know I have the power to put you to death?" and he quietly replied, "Yes, and I have the power to die and put you to shame." Yoga can produce such men, if it be aided by the other two practices of this yoga in daily life, namely, Self-study and Attentiveness to God. This brings us to the second practice, Self-study—or shall we call it philosophy?

2. *Self-study.* In the past I have often spoken and written of my definitions of science, religion and philosophy. In this view, science deals with things, religion with lives (hence its two departments of ethics in relation to men and animals, and devotion in relation to God), while philosophy is concerned with the relation between lives and things, and, particularly in any one person's case, between his life felt as within the body and his environment outside it. "What am I, and what

shall I do in my environment?" are the fundamental questions of philosophy. Let us not confuse philosophy with metaphysics, but revive the old idea of philosophy that was primarily concerned with the conduct of life. Such are the thoughts and outlook of the novice in yoga when he turns to the second part of his task, the practice of Self-study.

I wish to clarify this definition of philosophy as the science of the relation between myself and my environment, and speak of it as the relation between myself and "my world." There are three things to consider—not merely myself and the world, but myself, "my world" and "the world." It is only a small part of the world that can be called my world. It is that part of the world in which my game is played. The rest of that world is, in many overlapping parts, "my world" for the rest of the living beings of the world. My world also overlaps the "my world" of many other selves in parts, so that my game is played partly in collaboration with other selves, and an ethical relation thus arises among us, as well as the practical relation of my influence upon the various things in "my world" and their influence upon me.

Self-study is study and thought about myself and my world. What are these, and what is their relation? Patanjali does not lay down any precise system of belief on these points, but leaves the novice to his own meditations on the subject. In this way, the thought-power of the novice will exercise itself. This department of the work gives the novice ample scope for meditation and, says Patanjali (II, 44), it opens the door for intuitive contact with one's desired divinity.

The belief in such divinities is very general with the Hindus, and is also an implication of their thought about the ultimate purpose and attainment of yoga. They hold that the cream, so to speak, has been skimmed off human evolution all through the ages, so that there exist in the inner realms or world of reality beings who have been men but are now be-

yond the human stage. These beings have achieved the goal
of yoga in the past, have removed the covering of the light
for themselves, and now live in a superhuman condition. As
we remove or thin out the covering of the light by our philosophical reflections and meditations, we receive intuitions
which are often believed to be communications from the
world of light through the particular channel or contact of
our own family divinity there.

By "family" I mean type. We are, as it were, cast in different molds, belonging more especially to a particular portion
of the whole universal mind. This explains why some people
are most interested in science, others in religion, others in art
and so on. Each stands for something and expresses something unique, and as he opens to the light he is illuminated
from within by his own archetypal section or model for his
type.

A complete statement of this idea would lead to a long
description. I will make only a brief statement, and ask the
novice to reflect upon it, so as to open the door to intuitions.
We are not evolving in the sense of changing into something
else. We are only growing, in the sense that we can sustain
and appreciate more and more of the inner light. More and
more of reality becomes ours, so that we come nearer to our
divine archetype. The divine archetype is not a material form,
but is a living reality composed of all the divinities. As a
simile, imagine the growth of a tree. In this view, the tree
does not grow out of the seed, but the pressure of the archetype causes the growth, and the archetype becomes manifest
in the type. In a sense, the future tree causes the growth of
the seed, the sapling, and so on. All evolution is thus "emergent." There is nothing new under the sun.

Transfer this simile to the realm of mind, and you have a
picture of man becoming truly himself by "overcoming the
powers of darkness" or "removing the covering of the light."
In the process he becomes capable of sustaining more and

more light without being overwhelmed by it, and the illumination comes to him in the form of intuitions.

Some people obstruct the process for themselves by cultivating a mood of dependence. They look for a "desired divinity" in the form of an external teacher. They think of a human form, and ask for information, instruction and orders through such a form. But intuition is a direct thing.

Sometimes, indeed, people create such a form in their own minds as a permanent idea or focal center, and then the mind receives its intuitions through apparently spoken words of that form, which is considered to be clairvoyantly seen, or more often felt and heard. It is for this reason that it is sometimes said that the body of a Master is an illusion. The body is an illusion, but the Master may very well be there. This gives us an example of the way in which truth and error constantly mingle in human thought.

Entirely in line with this is the common Hindu practice of meditating upon what are called the "pictured ones." This will perhaps seem a curious idea to the Western mind, until it is understood. "The pictured ones" means the divinities which are represented in pictures on the walls of nearly every home. The picture is a focus for thought and meditation, but the meditator never must forget that the divinity is, as such, unpicturable, and the climax of his meditation is an alert expectancy of something beyond form, an awaiting of intuition unprejudiced by any made or pictured form. May I say that this is not altogether unlike the act of a little girl playing with a doll? She knows in her heart that the doll is not a real baby, but she gets all the good of it from within herself.

Let me ease this idea further into the mind of the Western novice by telling him that a cat may look at a king, but will not see a king, but only a man dressed up in a certain way. A man can see a king. If a novice tells me that he has met a Master and talked to a Master, I am reminded of this. Really he can only know the desired divinity by meeting him in the union of his nature with his. "He who lives the life will know the doctrine."

3. *Attentiveness to God.* We come now to the third concurrent practice of the triple yoga in active life, which will do for the novice's emotions what Body-conditioning and Self-study do for his body and his thought.

God, according to Patanjali (I, 24), is a particular soul, not affected by having a container of Sources of Trouble, karmas and fruition.

This calls for an explanation. A man is also a soul, or real man, and that soul is not a product—is not produced by anything or any other soul—and also is not a producer—does not make things. But he sits like a driver in the seat of a motor car and thus partakes of the troubles, doings and effects of the car.

I must write about the Sources of Trouble in the next chapter, but let me now say this much—that in human life our instinctive Sources of Trouble (which are all psychological —this is important) lead us on to actions or works, and these in turn lead to fruitions or results, which are our conditions of experience or environment. Sitting in that seat or affected by the "container," we become involved in this cycle, or series, or wheel of recurring causes. But that special and different soul whom we call God does not. He is unaffected by the world. He is called the powerful, not because He is ordering our lives and events, but because He rules himself and is not ruled by troubles, works or fruitions. His power is something to admire, to venerate, to emulate. In Him is the unexcelled source of all knowledge (I, 25) and He was the teacher also of the ancients, because not limited by time (I, 26).

What, then, are we to expect from Him? Certainly not any interference with our Sources of Trouble, karmas and fruitions. This will become abundantly clear when we come to the study of the Sources of Trouble in the next chapter. We are to expect the awakening of the power of contemplative intuition by Attentiveness to God.

Now—this is important—inasmuch as we shall have to practice contemplation with reference to all kinds of things, we must prostrate ourselves before God, the supreme teacher, in or through those things. And inasmuch as the novice is engaged in Attentiveness to God in the degree or grade of the yoga of daily life, he has to practice Attentiveness to God in reference to all things in daily life. The supreme teacher is everywhere.

Do not forget that this Attentiveness is a matter of feeling or emotion, just as Body-conditioning was a matter of will and Self-study was a matter of thought. I have had to describe Attentiveness to God intellectually—this being a book —but it is to be practiced emotionally. We all know what religious devotion is.

The religious mystics of all countries have shown us the nature of this devotion. One Hindu said to me: "What God does is best for us," when he missed his train. It is said that the sage is content with whatever comes to him outside his own effort. In modern parlance, he can find the good in everything. And he can find it the better if he faces without fretting what may seem to be bad, and best of all if he gives a glad welcome to all the lessons of his experience.

The point of this is that the supreme teacher is always teaching us, and if we will not approach Him through intuition, then He will still reach us through extuition—a new word which looks ugly at first. The operation is thus: (a) we perform an action (karma); (b) we thus make something (a karma); (c) that something some day ripens into our environment (called karma); (d) that environment, through pleasure and pain, teaches us. This tuition from the outside I have called extuition. It is something infinitely valuable, for the finite awakens the infinite in us. My experience, pleasurable or painful, does this for me if I receive it in the right spirit, with the full thankfulness of real emotional devotion.

You cannot force this devotion, but you can let it develop by this understanding, removing that covering of the light which is apt to manifest in our lives as discontent, resentment, impatience, envy, jealousy and all their brood, all of which will raise their ghostly arms and run shrieking away when we face them with the gaze that knows them for what they are. They cannot bear the light.

Is this a thing that we will remember sometimes and often forget? Patanjali has provided for that. He says: "His indicator is the sacred word" (I, 27). "It should be repeated with thought upon its meaning" (I, 28). And, "From that will come understanding of the individual consciousness and an absence of obstacles" (I, 29).

The sacred word is "OM." It is made up of three letters—A,U,M. The two vowels, *a* (sounded as *a* in "America") and *u* (sounded as *u* in "put") blend into *o* (sounded as *o* in "hope"). M is sounded as in English, with the lips closed, and no vowel inherent in it. In the word it has O before it, and no vowel after it, the lips remaining closed. The result sounds like "home" without the *h*, but prolonged impressively and with deep intent. It is considered more efficacious when repeated mentally than when repeated aloud. It is generally moderately prolonged, occupying the period of a slow out-breathing.

This word is considered to differ from all other words, in that their meanings are conventional but this has inherent meaning. The word "elephant" will signify a camel if we all agree that henceforth that shall be its meaning. But OM is made up thus: Open your mouth and, without moving any part of it, make the most elementary sound at the back of it. That sound will be "a," and you cannot make it different. At the other end of the scale or scientific alphabet you get "m," with the closing of the lips. All other letters arise from some position of the tongue, lips and teeth between these two. So OM is *the* complete word and the only suitable word to represent God, as it is the word which, if sufficiently prolonged, and glided without any jump from beginning to end, would be heard to contain all the articulate sounds of which we are capable. In this way it has some inherent capacity to remind us of the divine. It is used constantly in India. Often I receive letters from Hindu friends with the word OM written at the top of the paper.

The novice may have observed that in practicing the three requirements of yoga in daily life he attends to all three parts of his extrovert nature—the body, the thinking apparatus and the feelings. His object is to see that all three carry on their activities on right lines and therefore get themselves into good condition. The suggestion sometimes made, and already mentioned earlier, that the body should be severely treated, mortified or injured by austerities or asceticism, becomes ridiculous in the light of even a little understanding of yoga. That Patanjali could never have meant anything like that is clear from the way in which he extols its increased beauty, strength and brightness as a result of yoga practices—as we shall see further on in this book.

Another safeguard. It must not be thought that because these are called practices of yoga in active life, they are intended to prepare the way for leaving active life, to go and sit under a tree and meditate all the time. What is expected to happen in normal cases is that the meditation part of yoga —to which we shall come in due course—will occupy part of the day, and will be conducted in solitude, or at least in quietude, for it is quite possible to have that (when the intermediate practices of sitting, breathing and controlling the senses have been done to some extent) even when traveling in train or bus, or, in short, at any time when we are not called upon to take notice of other people.

In India, in the old days, when a man saw the arrival of

grandchildren, and when his son was ready to take over some of his work or business, he could make a partial retirement into a little house in the garden at the back of the large family house, and thus find more time than before for reading, thought, study and meditation. Even in the busy and very extrovert life of America an increase of the time given to these things, especially as we grow older, can make every kind of activity and experience richer and stronger. Time spent in concentration and meditation is not wasted, even from the external point of view, but is more than made up for by these effects.

Patanjali tells us that the triple yoga of daily life which I have described in this chapter has two uses:

II, 2. "It has the purposes of promoting Contemplation and causing reduction of the Sources of Trouble."

What the Sources of Trouble are we shall learn in the next chapter

CHAPTER 5

THE FIVE SOURCES OF TROUBLE

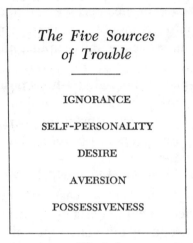

> *The Five Sources of Trouble*
> ———
> IGNORANCE
>
> SELF-PERSONALITY
>
> DESIRE
>
> AVERSION
>
> POSSESSIVENESS

Chart 4

All our troubles are psychological. Patanjali does not say this in so many words, but he describes the process clearly in various aphorisms. He says:

II, 3. "The Sources of Trouble are Ignorance, Self-personality, Desire, Aversion and Possessiveness."

What is the relation of these five Sources of Trouble to the five kinds of Ideas described in Chapter 2?

Some say the Sources of Trouble are forms of wrong knowledge, the second of the five Ideas. But they are not ideas. They are feelings, or rather, emotions. And they are instinctual, coming from a sub-human past. Let me explain.

In promoting yoga-knowledge and yoga-practice we may

think of four grades of men, whom I will call the mineral-man, the vegetable-man, the animal-man and the man-man, in order to make the distinctions clear.

The mineral-man, very numerous among us, is he who does not bestir himself without external cause. He would be content to lie on his back in the sunshine and allow the fruit of the trees to fall into his mouth if that were possible. He is devoid of ambition. He is mentally supine, but can do what he is taught.

The vegetable-man is more alive—he is pushing. But he is a weed, not cultivating himself, but pushing with that relentlessness which is characteristic of the coarse weeds of the jungle, which in a few years can cover and destroy deserted houses and even cities.

The animal-man is like an animal which, because it can run about, has learned to think, or at least to know a good many objects, to remember them under suitable stimulus and suggestion, and to recognize different types of situations and apply to them suitable types of behavior. Even a small puppy will generally look over the edge of a bank, and have the sense not to walk over it. The animals act by the operation of accumulated self-promoting ideas in their primitive minds, with a dawning faith in the constancy of Nature or law or order in the world. The animal-man lives in human society with cunning, adding obedience to natural law, as it is called, to the mineral pleasure and the vegetable pushfulness of mineral-man and vegetable-man.

Does this suggest a new sort of quiz, to test yourself to determine to which group you belong? Whichever it is, you must come out of it and become a man-man before you will care for yoga. What is the difference? The man-man cultivates himself. He is no longer subject to the law of natural selection.

As thinking man can take the wild flowers and cultivate them into the beauties of the garden, so the man-man governs his own life and cultivates himself. He does not leave his future to be the haphazard product and by-product of the struggle for existence. Well has it been said that truly human life begins where necessity leaves off. My Hindu friends call such a man a Brahmin, or god-man. They define him not by the caste of birth but by the caste of character, and say that he alone is ripe to become a candidate for the school of yoga. He is not really yet god-man, but he is fit to be a candidate for god-manship. Look now at your Sources of Trouble in the light of this understanding of man, and you will see that they are our inheritance from an inferior past, and that it is these emotions that have attached us to our bodies; whereas we should advance so as not to be attached to them but to be able to use them for truly human ends.

We will now take up Patanjali's definitions of these five troubles.

II, 5. *"Ignorance is regarding the non-eternal, impure, painful and not-self as the eternal, pure, pleasant and self."*

This is a very deep and habitual instinct, an unconscious emotional habit. But it is ignorance, humanly speaking. In the course of ages the animals and man have built this attitude or outlook into their subconscious systems; then, after the characteristically reflective life of man began, this outlook was continued. It is now to be overcome by thinking on the facts and seeing the truth of the matter.

Let me elucidate this a little. Early living forms had function without organs. When the amoeba wants to eat, it makes a temporary mouth. When it wants to move along, it pushes out primitive equivalents of tail and fin, and withdraws them when the purpose is attained.[1]

[1] In *Behaviour in the Lower Organisms*, Dr. Jennings has said: "If the amoeba were a large animal, so as to come within everyday experience of human beings, its behaviour would at once call forth the attribution to it of states of pleasure and pain, of hunger, desire and the like, on precisely the same basis as we attribute these things to a dog." I do not assume that Dr.

Gradually, in the course of what is called evolution, some of these actions become so frequent and so fixed that their effects in the body become permanent and structural. Now the fins and tail are carried about all the time by the fish, and very frequently used. This has advantages. In the human form, for example, the knees bend one way. They are always ready to do so on the instant. They became so formed to provide primitive man with the kind of instrument which suited what he was trying to do in his environment.

Such structures as knees are essentially habits. They are rightly described as "lapsed intelligence," because to use them we do not now need to do any conscious work. If men now decided to cease walking henceforth and, in preference, to wriggle along the ground on their abdomens, in course of time the knees would almost disappear and propulsive muscles somewhat resembling those of snakes would become part of the structure of the human body.[2] But, of course, man's body will not change much in the future, because man has reached that degree of intelligence by which he can adapt his environment to his body, and is no longer under the necessity of adapting his body to his environment.

Let us now return to the statement that the emotional and mental habit of regarding the not-self body as the self is a trouble, and an obstruction to correct or true man-man life. This affliction, as it has sometimes been called, is here being translated as "Ignorance."

When we speak of an ignorant man we do not mean an unconscious man, or even a man without knowledge. We mean a man acting ignorantly. In this case we mean a man

Jennings draws exactly the same conclusions as I do from this fact, but it is clear that the kind of intelligence that you and I attribute to a dog we are justified in attributing also to the amoeba. I remember that some scientific thinker once said: "Man and the mineral are brothers." My question then is: "Is man only an elaborated mineral, or is the mineral an undeveloped man?"

[2] Assuming, of course, that those who refused to submit to the new mode were prevented from propagating their species.

living ignorantly as regards himself. In yoga, we regard the body as not-self, and we learn to distinguish between the eternal and non-eternal, the pure and the impure, the pleasant and the painful.

Many civilized people have arrived in their personal life at a kind of negative happiness. Just as some people define peace as "not war," so do they feel satisfaction in a probable distantness of death, in the possession of clean houses and bathrooms, and in small pleasures, such as playing cards. But they have not anything that can even distantly be called bliss. The yogī says: "Open your eyes to this fact. To one who knows the truth about life your condition seems miserable."

It is the condition of the animal-man, however refined. If you observe and remember that this is a state of error, you thereby become a man-man. But do not be unkind to yourself. Our object in the first grade of yoga practice is to weaken, not to destroy, the Sources of Trouble. You must not even dwell in thought upon the idea that some day you will destroy them. At every stage we have to attend strictly to present business. Do not even perform the three practices of Body-conditioning, Self-study and Attentiveness to God with the thought: "I am doing this to weaken the Sources of Trouble." You must perform those three with delight in the life of performing them, and the weakening of the Sources of Trouble will proceed by itself. There is no harm, however, in knowing that the weakening of the Sources of Trouble does and will occur.

We will now consider for a moment the pairs of opposites mentioned in this aphorism (II, 5). The eternal is ascribed to the temporary. This occurs in a variety of ways. The environment of a man, that is, the "world," is habitually regarded as permanent or eternal—changing form, yes, but not changing substance or reality. Why? Where did man get this idea of eternity? From himself, because he felt and found in himself something unchanging among the changing. He thought of himself as the same self today and yesterday and, by anticipatory thought, tomorrow.

Primitive man, said Professor Thomas H. Huxley, the famous naturalist, did not know of natural death, nor think that his bodily structure contained the seeds of its own destruction. Even now, though we are no longer primitive, it is worth while to reflect that it is only the structure that dies. Primitive man knew of death. It was occurring every now and then. But he ascribed it to accident, killing or black magic—not to a natural process. It was related of one primitive tribe that such was their childishness that when one of their elders became very old, helpless and a nuisance, they would carry him into the jungle, lay him there, go away a little distance, look, pretend that they saw a deer, shoot the supposed deer to death with arrows, then run up and discover with many lamentations that they had accidentally killed the old man. Killed the old man? No, not quite that, for they still thought of him as going on, in some other sort of body, in some other sort of world.

Body and world—aye, there's the rub. Men think that in themselves eternity can lie. Even today, if they can obtain evidence by some kind of psychic research or spiritualism that after death there exists a material body of a finer kind and that it resembles the dead body left behind, they think they have attained some scientific knowledge of human immortality. They would find it difficult to believe in immortality without form, in pure consciousness, seeing without any sort of eyes, and hearing without any sort of ears, or in a sort of consciousness which is seeing and more than seeing and hearing and more than hearing, and a reality which is of time and more than time, and is of space and more than space. The true immortality conception must be more, not less. In this light the body is less than man. In him lies the eternity.

I must not leave this subject without a brief statement that man manifests that eternity. Waves of light enter the eye. In the man there is sensation—quite a different thing. In man there is something that bridges time. Notes played separately are to him music, because in his consciousness he can take a handful of time. He is superior to time. He thinks, and plans, and makes forms, and breaks forms. Indeed, he and his cogeners, the animals, the vegetables and the amoeba, and even the minerals in their lesser power, make all forms and worlds and endow them with time and space. People say: "If a man dies, the world remains." True, and if all men died perhaps the animals, the vegetables and the minerals would remain, but the cities and bridges and cultivated fields would go. If then the animals, the vegetables and the minerals also all died one would expect the world to go still further back into some yet simpler or more elemental form of the expression of life. We have no logical or evidential ground for the assumption that the world is in any sense eternal.

In his ethical nature, as well as in his thought, man is superior to forms, for it is true that human beings can love one another and that when souls reach a certain height they manifest a law above selfishness, something that bridges space and does not acknowledge dependence on the spatial form that is the body. In the will, too, men manifest their allegiance to a superior state, when they prefer death to dishonor or slavery.

So much for taking the non-eternal to be the eternal, the temporary to be the permanent, the sequence to be the enveloping causality which is the background of all.

A little study of the nature of causality will help us here. Really, causality is not just regular or invariable sequence—that B always follows A. B does follow A, but A is not therefore the cause of B. Night follows day, and day follows night, but night is not the cause of day, nor day the cause of night. The cause is something enveloping and covering both—the rotation of the earth in relation to the sun. Bricks are not the cause of houses, and atoms are not the cause of bricks, and electrons are not the cause of atoms. We must say, I think, that only "the whole" is the cause of everything. Nothing is itself except in relation to that.

Next we come to the mistaking of the impure for the pure. It has been said by an old writer of India: "Because of the necessity of keeping the body clean, and because of its condition, its origin, its mode of maintenance, its sweat and its decay, thoughtful people regard it as unclean." And yet, it is added, people see purity in that. "The young woman is lovely like the new moon. Her limbs seem as if made of honey and nectar. She looks as though having broken open the moon she has stepped out from it. With playful glances of her eyes which are large like the leaves of the lotus she delights the world of beings."

I remember that in one of David Hume's essays he remarked that if the young man would take a microscope to inspect his lady-love he would be repelled rather than attracted by her. Is the object here to create a disgust for the body? That cannot be, in true yoga, for this idea is itself disgusting, and is therefore itself impure. Our object is to realize the pure. From where shall we draw that idea?

We know that beauty is only skin deep, but who wants it to be otherwise? That beauty is immensely lovable, but it is not really of this earth. It is only *manifest* through the form. It is emergent reality. Furthermore, it is to some extent in the eye of the beholder. The body is non-eternal, and also impure. "Let it be known," some of my yogī friends might say, "that even if there is beauty it is not *in* that. You are seeing through the form, or, better, using the form as an instrument for your own self-revelation."

I like the simile of the child with the doll, which I mentioned in Chapter 4. The make-believe is good for the child. I like, too, the way in which the great teacher Shankarāchārya, in one of his commentaries, permits the devotee to meditate upon the pictures or images of deity with all their complexity of symbolical detail—provided the worshiper remembers in the back of his mind that there is no such real thing. Shankarāchārya, as is well known, was the philosopher who, above all, warned us against any attempt to think of the ultimate reality in terms of what we now know.

I would go so far in this as to confront the aspirant with the alarming statement that there is no reality, meaning that even his conception "reality" is unreal. I will not say, however, that we must ultimately expect something else, because by that thought we err in the opposite direction. The point is that thought is not the instrument for knowledge of reality. The whole aim of yoga is to go beyond thought. But I ask the aspirant at this point not to clamp down even on this idea, for having gone beyond thought, he might now make the mistake of thinking that thought will go into the discard, if I did not issue this warning. I will write more about this further on, in a more appropriate place. Let me here only safeguard the beauty of which I wrote above, and say it is to be regarded similarly. Such beauty is for the man-man; but for the god-man, what? We shall see.

Ascribing pleasurableness to the painful remains to be discussed. The pleasures of the body are definitely limited in their range. A warm bath is pleasant; let the water be much hotter or much colder and it will be painful. We cannot fully enjoy any of our physical pleasures, remarked one Hindu writer, for while we are doing so, we reflect that we cannot have more of it, and also that it will come to an end. "Our sincerest laughter," wrote the poet Shelley, "with some pain is fraught." Visitors to India sometimes learn to eat with pleasure food which contains such hot spices that it inflicts considerable pain upon the novice. I do not know whether that ever becomes really enjoyable, but suspect that it is only the stimulus or excitement which passes for pleasure. Perhaps it is really a sort of pain, which is liked because it convinces the moribund person that he is alive; a mild masochism. But that there is pleasure of the body is certainly known from observing the actions of animals—the cat when it relaxes itself in the sunshine or before the fire, the dog when it goes for a walk, the race horse when it stretches its limbs in full gallop. For man there are generally few pleasures of this kind, except in the young, as he has so much spoiled them by excess, but for him there are the pleasures of the mind—of thought and love, and the will. Patanjali warns us against taking pleasure in the painful, and tells us it is a part of our trouble of ignorance.

We come to the second Source of Trouble. Patanjali says:

II, 6. *"Self-personality is the unification, as it were, of the Looker and the instrument of looking."*

Even when a man does not think of himself as the body, he often identifies himself with his mind—the instrument or power of seeing. I call this Self-personality, because personality is a man's instrument in the world. We have to distinguish three things—the world, my world and myself—as mentioned before. I must now observe what my personality is in my world. I may consider first the body which has grown up from babyhood in a certain way and under certain conditions. At first that little child did not know itself as an entity, but it had definite character. When, inadvertently, you stuck a pin into it, there was a decided conscious reaction. It felt the prick of the pin and it knew it felt it, but it did not *think* what it was that knew it and felt it.

Gradually, however, the child came to distinguish clearly between itself and other persons and objects. Gradually it acquired more and more ideas about itself. It saw itself in mirrors. It found itself possessing certain powers—there were certain things it could do and certain others which it could not. It began to understand language, and heard itself spoken of as clever or stupid, as strong or weak, as good- or bad-tempered. It went to school and college. It became adolescent and, entering more and more into new situations in adult society, it felt uncomfortable and acted awkwardly, because it did not know how it would be accepted in that society.

Thus it was with each of us. Time went on and our young man or woman settled into his or her profession. Then he or she was accepted as such-and-such and acted as such-and-such, and thus the personality became matured, with definite powers and limitations. The personality was now an instrument for playing "my game." It saw and felt, planned and acted. It became a useful and even a necessary thing; for an unformed personality, brought up in the jungle and unrelated to contemporary society, would be entirely unadapted to play "my game" in the modern social world.

Now, the question for each of us is: "Have I Self-personality? Do I regard that personality instinctively as myself—if not the body, at least the habitual emotions, and the collection of ideas which also form part of it?"

"In some degree or at some times I do," will be the answer. To that extent you have Self-personality, will be the verdict. The three practices of Body-conditioning, Self-study and Attentiveness to God will gradually weaken that trouble, and ultimately yoga will remove it altogether. At present we are concerned only with its weakening.

But, be it observed, there is no proposal to weaken the personality, or to injure it in any way. To do that would be another form of the error of the misguided and partially insane would-be yogīs who torture and maim their bodies in order to demonstrate their powers to themselves, or, as Sir Edwin Arnold put it in *The Light of Asia,* perchance in the depths of their ignorant fear of the future, "to baulk hell by self-kindled hells."

On the third of the Sources of Trouble Patanjali pronounces as follows, showing how desire often governs our actions, through memory, imagination and thought.

II, 7. "Desire is a follower of pleasure."

The word here translated desire (*rāga*) is more psychologically revealing than its English equivalent. It implies that the idea of the thing desired is coloring the mind, on account of memory of the pleasure it gave, or anticipation of the pleasure it is expected to give. The word means "color," and it is used for "dye" in the making of cloth. Here it means that you are colored by your environment. Instead of calmly playing your game of life, you very largely allow it to play you.

Certain agitating emotions arise in this situation (particularly fear, anger and pride), and these throw your powers of thought, love and will quite out of gear for the time being. When you are agitated by these you cannot do anything with calm judgment. You are driving a car and you see there is about to be a collision with another car. Fear springs up and prevents that instant decision to act with judgment, which might avert it. Examination day approaches, and the unlucky student spends the night before it in trying to make up some deficiency, but he cannot grasp his subject because his mind is occupied by thoughts of success and failure.

Fear is useful for the animals, and perhaps for the mineral-man and the vegetable-man, but not for the man-man. Caution and forethought are his sublimations of this instinct. In the animal, fear acts on the adrenal glands and prepares the organism to put forth extra energy in fight or flight; but man has to overcome his difficulties by careful thought. Anger arises when an obstacle stands in the way. It, too, obstructs thought. Similarly pride, when feelings are "hurt."

The chief instinct in this group, however, is plain Desire. The man sees something and wants it. It colors his life. It drives him. His doings are not decided from within by calm judgment, but are governed by this limited thing that he desires. Very fanciful things often come in here, like the case of the man who went in for golf, not because he liked golf but because he wanted to display his calves, and therefore to wear the knickerbockers which were worn in his day by men when golfing. What are called personal fetishes also come in here, sometimes connected with sex. A discussion of those would be out of place here. Let me only say that fancies and fads and whims and personal fetishes are often harmless to the person and to others, and that it is not desirable in that case to upset the psychological balance of a personality by repressing them.

As in the treatment of a pet animal, the mind must be sufficiently indulged to secure its smooth functioning, and the outlet of unbalanced personal energies or habits of thought. There is a good deal of fetishism in modern psychological pictures; they contain plenty of instruction, and in certain ways relief for the artist (unless he builds them up as a convention, that is, for ulterior social motives), but for beauty we must look only at pieces of them in detail, as beauty lies in the organic manifestation of the will, which is not represented here.

In all cases it is to be remembered that Body-conditioning, Self-study and Attentiveness to God will effect the weakening of this Source of Trouble also, without any direct action.

Patanjali's aphorism defining the fourth of the Sources of Trouble is:

II, 8. "Aversion is a follower of pain."

This again is a form of being colored or driven from outside. Considerable human activity is dictated by the desire to get away from something or somebody, or to avoid pain in some form. If this occupies the mind when it ought to be calmly sizing up a situation and deciding what things are really good and bad, and for what purpose, and what can be done in the circumstances, it is so much loss of true living. A lot of worry comes in here.

The Stoics had a good formula in reference to this. Their idea was that we should not occupy our minds with things we cannot control or alter, but should decide to think, and to act, only with reference to what is in our power. Generally speaking, this Aversion or hatred operates principally when the disliked or painful object is not in our power. If we have the power, we either suppress the object or escape from it, and then the hatred dies down. But if it is not in our power and yet we dwell upon it with dislike, or loathing or repulsion, these agitating emotions spoil the operations of our mental life. If, however, we are practicing Body-conditioning, Self-study and Attentiveness to God, all this trouble will soon quite naturally fade into a shade of its present strength.

Patanjali thus defines and describes the fifth and last of the Sources of Trouble:

II, 9. *"Possessiveness, which is firmly established even in the learned, carries on by its own relish."*

Perhaps the most physical or least mental of all these troublous instincts is Possessiveness, which in its broadest form is seen in clinging to life. This is an inborn and continuous impulse, not dependent, as Desire and Aversion are, on pleasure and pain.

We used to define the difference between non-living and living forms by reference to the instinct of self-preservation. As evolution advances, it is seen to be more than self-preservation. Self-expansion becomes evident. It is not merely clinging to life, but also desire for more life. It has made grubs into butterflies and kings into emperors. It makes young men fight and old men hold on to remnants of physical capacity. It makes young women dress up, and converts talent into genius. It makes the exhibitionist and the proud, aloof hermit. Even a worm just born, it is said, has the fear of death, as does the most learned man. Here again we have something useful to the mineral-man, the vegetable-man and the animal-man, but something to be weakened in the man-man, and to disappear in the god-man.

Such is the subtlety of this possessiveness that it may sometimes be seen even in suicide. "I shall be greater or freer in death than in life," or, "I shall herein manifest my power over the body." This is not the "open door" of the Stoic, who said that no one has a right to complain about his life, since the door is always open for him to leave it, and it is illogical for him to stay voluntarily and then complain.

It is responsible, too, for numerous subconscious suicides, in which perverted expansionism drives their victims to the satisfaction of experiences which involve their death—ranging from the desire for the experience of falling from a height that grows into a compelling thought-picture and results in a leap into space, to a great number of apparently unintentional pedestrian suicides under the wheels of traffic.

Ordinary clinging to possessions comes into this trouble-group. It is enough to say that when we possess, we are also possessed. It is useful to be able to see, with reference to a particular thing we own, whether we possess it more than it possesses us, or it possesses us more than we possess it. In the latter case, loss of the object would really be a gain. The carpenter must have his tools and must look after them, but he who keeps tools not required for use loses his own liberty to some extent. This applies to everything, including the body.

Often this clinging to forms causes a deeper clinging to personality. We must wear a certain type of clothing and dwell in a certain kind of house, it may be for a useful status in the world or it may be subjectively, to preserve a definite sense of oneself. "I am a doctor," says one, and he not only lives in that idea but also plays the part in appearance and mannerisms. If we are something, we do not mind not being something else, but we cling to the something as our very life. "Without my parrots," said one observant lady, "I should hardly know myself."

Patanjali said that the last four Sources of Trouble are within the first one—Ignorance. The aphorism reads:

II, 4. "*Ignorance is the field for all the others, whether they be (at any given time) dormant, slight, obstructed or vigorous.*"

That all the Sources of Trouble are forms of Ignorance is easy to see. Now we have something further to think about them, which is in line with some of the modern psychological probings into the "unconscious" or "subconscious." The Sources of Trouble may be for a time inactive or sleeping. They may be slight even to the point of being unnoticed. They may be blocked or suppressed. But they are still there. In contrast to these three states, they may be uplifted, vigorous and flourishing. Sometimes one is temporarily cut off or obscured by another, as when a mother is angry with her little boy who has been naughty, but suddenly loses her anger in a wave of love.

All the Sources of Trouble are at bottom so subtle or fine that you cannot find the root of them. They are not defects or sins or psychological diseases, but have arisen from some deep need of ours for experience. Nevertheless, to pass from our present state of man-manship to our fulfillment in god-manship, we have to overcome them or allow them to fall into desuetude through our knowing them for what they are. They wither in the light of truth—true seeing, feeling and action in life. That is why, in II, 2, Patanjali prescribed the yoga of daily life to weaken them. The three practices of Body-conditioning, Self-study and Attentiveness to God generate the contrary of the Sources of Trouble by substituting a new motive in life which weakens and replaces them. Their obvious manifestations—the motive in most of the business in people's lives—are to be seen with a little thought. Meditation on these is enough to cause them to fall away. These principles are enunciated by Patanjali in two aphorisms:

II, 10. *"These (Sources of Trouble), when subtle, are removable by the generation of their contraries."*
II, 11. *"Their forms (in expression) are removable by Meditation."*

When truly human motives replace these instincts in our minds, these Sources of Trouble will be burnt out, as it were, even to their roots. As to their expressions manifest in our lives—after they have been weakened, Meditation will complete our release from their sway, as further chapters will show.

CHAPTER 6

THE MAN AND HIS BODY

In his Book II, aphorisms 12 to 27, Patanjali presents us with his theory of life, that is, of the relation between a man, his body, his world and the world. To begin at the beginning, with birth, he says:

II, 12. *"The karma-container has its root in the Sources of Trouble and is experienced in seen and unseen births."*

The karma-container is more than the visible body, which expresses only a part of our karma. It is the receptacle of our karmas, latent as well as active. From it the visible body arises as a fructification or ripening of a group of our karmas.

II, 13. *"The root being there, it ripens into life-condition, length of life and experience."*

II, 14. *"These fructify in joy and grief, caused by virtue and vice."*

The karma-container or seat of habit-molds and karmas is, in full fruition, what we call the body and experience. Similarly, we would speak of the mind as the seat of thought. With the body we perform actions in our world, but the word karma goes further than that. It is an ancient and universal belief among the Hindus that karma means also the results of actions, or work done, and that those results cling to their maker and reappear as experience. Thus, if a carpenter makes a chair, both the action and the chair are karma. If I inflict pain on a dog, both the action and the pain are karmas. Further, they are my karmas, and coming into the body, or being born and growing up, I will some time have to meet that karma of cruelty and experience something of the kind my-self. Suppose the carpenter is a bad workman and he makes uncomfortable chairs. His karma may not be to have to sit in uncomfortable chairs, but it will be that he must experience in some way the discomfort that he has made, perhaps in the form of uncomfortable clothes or an uncomfortable bed.

The theory of karma allows for social intercourse and collective work. The carpenter was not entirely responsible for the chair; other people worked to obtain the wood for it, and others again furnished him with tools necessary for the work. "My world" overlaps and mingles with portions of the "my worlds" of many people. Our karmas are also largely collective. We experience many things together. The division of labor and sharing of its products are endlessly complicated, but the belief is that each person gets some equivalent of the experience he has given to others, both good and bad. Virtue or goodness leads to joy, and vice to grief-laden experience. No one experiences anything but his karma, so it will be in order to say that "my world" is my karma, "your world" is your karma, and the whole world of forms is composed of the karmas of all the beings living in the world in all their bodies, and is nothing but that. We are many beings in one world because we have our social feelings and social actions and do a great deal of varied work together. Our feelings bring us together socially and our work brings us together in one big collection of products which we call the world.

The fact that we could not be what we are except together points to a basic principle of unity. I cannot imagine anyone living in a void and at the same time being of sound mind, even if by some miracle he could be kept alive. There is no need, however, to push imagination so far, for we all know that other people, and animals and plants, and rocks and the very soil, air and sky have gone into our minds and are needed there. Our social existence, bodily and mental, has therefore become mainly selective. The young lady goes into the department store, and can be clad from head to foot and provided with everything she needs for her home, but she has selected and combined all these things of her choice in accordance with her character. She comes out not only with things in her hands, but also with things in her mind derived from what she has seen and heard and the pleasant and unpleasant human contacts she has had. And we presume that sometime and somewhere she will work with her brain and hands to make her contribution to this great panorama of give and take. If she has virtue she will want to do so, at all events. There is a deep need in us that makes us want to give as well as take. From these considerations it is not a far cry to the thought that all our virtues and vices towards one another will somehow sooner or later be balanced up—it is what we want in our hearts, to be socially clean, and happy together. Our Hindu friends resolved this thought many centuries ago into the ideas of reincarnation and karma, but yoga practice stands as psychologically sound whether these be true to fact or not.

The body, Patanjali tells us, arises from the Sources of Trouble. This means that all the karmas are due ultimately to these five instinctual emotions—Ignorance, Self-personality, Desire, Aversion and Possessiveness. These impulses, Patanjali tells us, are the causes of incarnation, and they take us to what we have attached ourselves to by similar impulses in past lives. This root being there, the body grows up and ripens in its economic class or social position destined by karma (modified by present efforts, of course), lives for a certain length of life and meets with certain kinds of experience.

The life-condition referred to is the objective basis of the personality of which I have already written. In ancient India it would have been definitely thought of in reference to caste, as in those days it almost invariably happened that sons followed their fathers' professions, generation after generation.

Caste was, in fact, mainly a social institution designed for stability, and in some respects it resembled the guild system and even our modern trade unions. Sons not only followed in their fathers' footsteps, but even usually lived in the ancestral home and when they married brought their wives there also. I remember when I was new to India and was visiting a village, I asked one young man how long he had been living there, and he replied quite casually, "Oh, I think probably about five thousand years," meaning that he thought the family had carried on in the same house (with repairs, of course!) for about that period. He was a cultivator. Other castes of old time, now dying rapidly away, as such, were the merchants, the soldiers, and the clerks and clerics, while those who did the unclean work were usually ranked as altogether outside caste. These groups mingle more than they used to do, and young men change their occupations to meet the opportunities of the new science and the new social world-order. When Patanjali spoke of life-condition he was thinking of such ideas as these. Briefly, we are born into the social environment and kind of body and family provided by our karmas.

Life-period refers to a common belief among the Hindus that we are each destined for a certain length of life, according to our karma, but this is generally considered to be alterable (as indeed status also is) by means of our current actions. There is always present activity to be taken into account, and what has sometimes been called "ready-money karma." If in a busy town a man crosses the street against the red light, in defiance or through neglect of the traffic regulations, any injury he may sustain must be credited to his present action as ready-money karma, not to karma coming over from a previous life. Similarly, good deeds done now with a good heart may counterbalance or neutralize certain outstanding karmas, or offset karmas which are in store and have not yet begun to fructify.

Experience refers to all the details of experience, effects of karma to be met during the coming lifetime.

In aphorism II, 12 cited earlier, Patanjali speaks of seen and unseen births. At this distance of time no one can say for certain whether he was thinking of future births, but that is most probable. Some have suggested that he may have meant hells or heavens. I adhere to the former view, for the following reasons. At death the body is thrown off and after a longer or shorter time the man returns to another bodily birth through the effect of his Sources of Trouble. In the new body he is brought in touch with a collection of things which are his own works of the past incarnation or incarnations. Such is his environment, including his body, and he now meets these as "his world," and acts with reference to all these things not from the pure center of his soul, so to speak, but again through his Sources of Trouble, which cover up the true light in him. So again he makes new karmas. The essence of the matter is that *this* is the world of karmas—the place of making and of meeting karmas.

In the light of this central statement, it cannot be said that after death a man goes to some other world to meet and deal with his karmas. If it were so, there would be no need for reincarnation. It would be illogical to think that karma could be dealt with twice over, in such different ways. To stay a while out of incarnation in a subjective condition, digesting his previous experiences into character would, however, be quite a different matter. These old stories of hells were evidently invented, as in Europe, to frighten people away from wickedness and tempt them into good conduct.

Aphorism II, 14 emphasizes the nature of karma as described above. Actions are due to Sources of Trouble and in turn lead to the fruition of actions or works in karmic experiences throughout life, and these are joyous or grievous according to their origins in virtue and vice. The new feature introduced in this aphorism is the statement about virtue and vice. Virtue leads to joy; vice to grief.

What is virtue, and what is vice? Virtue is living according to reason, love and self-government. It is living from within. Take the body first. To give it housing, food, clothing, exercise, work, rest and amusement, all in the amount indicated by the laws of health and your own idiosyncrasies, is virtue. Then the outposts of the body—your beds, couches, chairs, tables, shelves, curtains, carpets, windows, living room, kitchen, bathroom, storeroom, garden and the rest—to have these orderly, well-proportioned, harmonious, healthy and useful is virtue. Then the surroundings—good air, sufficient quietude, natural beauty and good company (including books) in moderation; to plan for all these in reasonable measure is virtue.

The supreme test of virtue in these is their organic unity or combinational simplicity—not paucity, but the fulfillment of one will, yours, in producing one harmonious unit of physical living. The inward test of success in this will be your peace and freedom from friction and obstacles. The outward test, beauty. Beauty is the final measure and touchstone of physical virtue, as joy is of the mental. It includes health.

Virtue with reference to other people is love. It is virtue to pause when dealing with other people and ask oneself what is going on in their minds, to think of their pleasures and pains, their hopes and fears, their opportunities and frustrations. It is not only judgment that is required, but perception by feeling. It is not acquiescence in their wishes that is required, but fellow-feeling. It is not living or directing their life that is required, nor even adapting your life to theirs, but it is having your own life self-governed, harmonious and beautiful—a good element in their environment. It is the proper recognition of our joint living in one world, and the fellow-feeling and neighborliness that knows where your life ends and his begins, and where and how they fit together and overlap. Primarily, it is love to want only your own share according to your own work, and to rejoice in your neighbor's success and possessions—in his happiness—as much as in your own. Is it extravagant if I say that though I may have no motor car and must do quite a lot of toiling on foot amid the dust, when I see my neighbor riding past in his Cadillac I am happy in him? There is much virtue in that life which Buddha extolled, which has been described as "like soft airs passing by."

Virtue leads to joy, says Patanjali. It surely does. And now vice? It needs no description, whether it be in the body and its outposts, or socially. It leads to grief. It is compounded fundamentally of idleness, selfishness and thoughtlessness, the negation of living, and therefore it necessarily leads to the obstructed life. These vices are a surrender to circumstances and an acceptance of their dictatorship, a voluntary slavery to events, not making happiness but working only for pleasure and to avoid pain.

Joy and grief can be immediate, felt now in our mind and character, or they can be indirect, coming at us through our karmas—or, we may say, there is outward joy and inward joy, and in valuing the latter we need not undervalue the former. Our joy and our grief, it will be noted, are not karmas, but are our inward states, resulting from our virtue and vice, that is, from the way we regard and deal with our environment or karma, whatever its nature may be.

I have now to quote an aphorism from Patanjali which seems to run counter to this, and I will take issue with him if necessary, though perhaps we shall, after all, find a fundamental agreement even in this. He says:

II, 15. *"Everything is painful to the discriminating person, because of transformation, worry, and habit-mold, and because of obstruction by the formations in the Qualities of Nature."*

To understand this aphorism we must read it in conjunction with the previous one. There the teacher said that the conditions of our bodily life are pleasurable if caused by virtue and painful if caused by vice. Aphorism II, 14 refers to the theory of karma, but with special reference to virtue and vice. It states that our good deeds will make pleasurable conditions and our bad deeds painful conditions in future lives. A good deed done now may not make for immediately pleasurable results, because it effects may mingle with the results of bad deeds done in the past of the present life and in past lives. Similarly, a bad deed done now may not produce painful results at once because of their obscuration or obstruction by the effect of good deeds from the past. This complication is not held to operate necessarily in all cases, "ready-money" karma being quite possible and, indeed, not infrequent. The central idea in all cases is that every man will get exactly what he deserves of pleasurable and painful experience—whatever he has sown he will reap, neither more nor less.

So it appears; but, he now adds, in Aphorism II, 15, if you look at it closely you will find that really all experiences are painful. Look at our life-state, life-time and life-experience, he seems to say. Even the best of them brings us pain. People enjoy those pleasures derived from meritorious actions, says he, as long as they are unthinking, but to the observant all are seen to be painful. It really means that the discerning man will not be satisfied with any of the very limited pleasures possible in our bodily life, because he thinks of something much better. It is a matter of relativity.

The man-man enters, it appears, upon a path of woe. The symbolism of the Christ-story bears the same lesson. The man-man finds himself stretched on the cross of matter. In him, surely enough, the God-man or christos will come to birth. Yoga also promises that, and prescribes for a living freedom.

Turning now to the latter part of the aphorism, I will first deal with the technicalities. The fundamental Qualities or properties of Nature are always spoken of as three, which are held to be at the very basis of material things, behind and inherent in all atoms and combinations of atoms. It is very interesting that the ancient Hindus hit upon the three things which are taken as fundamental in Nature by the modern scientist, namely, matter, energy and law. These are the real elements of consideration in all the study of external Nature. We study (a) material objects; (b) the forces of Nature; and (c) that orderliness and constancy of properties and action which we classify as natural law.

Among the Hindus these were regarded not as three separate realities, but as three aspects of one reality—some kind of root-matter or substance. All forms were held to possess and exhibit different proportions of these three elements. A thing or person was spoken of as predominantly material if inert or sluggish; as restless if overactive and energetic; and as harmonious if orderly and law-considering. All objective things are forms composed of the Qualities of Nature and—observe the ancient science here moving into the realm of psychology—are obstructions in human life.

In some of my writings I have spoken of the external or material world as the world of obstruction. Our body needs these obstructions, but they are nevertheless irksome, and in some degree therefore always painful. For example, we want to walk. For that we need the obstruction offered us by the ground; otherwise we should be like persons pedaling on bicycles without chains and not moving along at all. Again, we wish to see, and we open our eyes. We cannot see through the wall of the room to what is beyond, so we see the wall. If the wall were perfectly transparent or unobstructive to the agencies of our sight, we could not see the wall. So, we move because we cannot move, and we see because we cannot see. The forms composed of and expressing the Qualities or fundamentals of Nature, namely matter, energy and law, stand in the way.

This is not an ideal existence, is it? We can think of floating through the air without effort, or reaching the goal of a journey by merely wishing to be there. Or we can think of an ideal seeing-organism by which we might focus sight just where we like, so that we could at will see what is on the other side of the wall without the trouble of getting up and walking through the door and around to the other side.

Our modes of personal motion and perception thus obviously involve resistance and some trouble, that is, at least a little pain. It is easy to see how one who thinks carefully and discriminates can class all these efforts of ours as troublesome and therefore painful. Having done that, a man may try to find his way, by some practice of yoga, into the world of pure unobstructed life, and he may very well say to himself: "I will not be tempted to linger in the pleasure-gardens of the human senses. I have pierced the illusoriness of those pleasures and will seek a superior goal."

What Patanjali does not mention is that there is pleasure with the pain, that the acts of moving and seeing involve some degree of the play of life and there is pleasure in that degree. The earth does not entirely obstruct our motion and the wall does not rebut our vision altogether. Let us enjoy those pleasures, for half a loaf is better than no bread, even though the quality of the half-loaf is not as good as the imagined quality of the whole.

Without looking at any ultimates, I do not doubt that this limitation by forms is in true harmony with the stage of unfoldment of our powers. The faith that is expressed in the very idea of Attentiveness to God really advertises this truth. To receive these obstructions or limitations with reverence, or at least with the most respectful consideration, is also a matter of discrimination and happy acceptance. When such acceptance is carried to a point of high perception and understanding, we shall find that, while the objects of the world obstruct us, they also educate, and we begin to learn the supernal truth that the infinite can manifest itself to us through the finite experience.

I know what Patanjali means, and that he does not disagree with all this. He means that all things are painful when the Sources of Trouble stand between them and us, and they are received and responded to through those channels. They then lead us into a wrong obedience, in which man is no longer master, either of things or of himself.

The fact is that we rightly live at the surface of things. Our truth, like our beauty, is only skin deep. Yet there is nothing in this fact to be despondent about. Our business is mainly with all kinds of forms, which we make and arrange, and rearrange, and also unmake or destroy. Outside of these, we deal with forms of the animal, vegetable and mineral orders —these also being superficial. It is not our business, apparently, to leave this surface and live among the electrons or perhaps among some billion-billionth substratum of those. And it is well so, for in this sphere of ours we have just what we need for the use of our faculties and powers. I would rather walk gracefully, putting my foot just to the ground and no more, than spend my time in study of the minutiae of the unseen inside parts of legs and feet. It is enough that these organs of ours obey our minds, and the result is obviously good for both.

One point more on this subject. It is well known that there are certain ganglia or nerve plexuses in the body (e.g. the cavernous, laryngeal, pharyngeal, cardiac, epigastric, prostatic and sacral) which carry on the functions of the organic life of the body without any will or thought of ours. In the far past they were no doubt within the cognitional sphere of consciousness, but gradually they were handed over to the unconscious, or sympathetic system. Some yogīs meditate upon these, and thereby bring them again within the cognitive or brain-center system, and then they can recover control of the workings of the heart, intestines and other viscera of the body, but in this there is no real gain.

Patanjali speaks also of the pains of change or transformation, worry, and habit-mold. Here again are some technicalities to be explained. There is no objection to change in itself. The trouble is that we fear change. We cannot really enjoy anything, because even while we have it we feel, in the words of Shakespeare, that "Time will come and take my love away." With perfect perspicuity Shakespeare continued: "This thought is as a death, which cannot choose but weep to have that which it fears to lose."

It is a fault of the world, is it not, that it fails to offer permanence in things for which we have striven, which we have obtained and liked? The discriminating person, says Patanjali, cannot find satisfaction in things which are transient. The object of delight changes, the body changes, and even the senses change. Even the mind changes its point of view. There are changes in the life-experiences and in the life-states, and these give us pain.

Next to change comes the thought of the constant worry even the pleasurable things give us. Suppose I have a nice garden beside my house, with a swimming pool and chairs for sitting on the lawn. I have the effort and indeed the worry of maintaining them. All things hurt us to some extent. They create anxiety in our minds, and at the same time they wear us down physically, even though they are pleasurable. You cannot deal with any of them without an effort to keep them, which is pain.

And after all this, when they are gone, the things still leave their marks upon us, impressions which awaken and give rise to new pains. Some of these residual effects are actually in the body, leaving us crippled and infirm; some in the mind, leaving heartaches, regrets, sorrows, hopes and subconscious intentions which spring into new life when opportunity offers, and start the wheel going all over again. "Hope springs eternal in the human breast." We have lost, we say, but we will gain. The seed dropped by the dead flower remains in us as habit-mold and will bring us, through our ignorance and the other four Sources of Trouble, back again to a new life-time, with its new state and new experiences and new round of pain.

I must explain a little more these marks or impressions left upon us. They are, as it were, the molds of our future actions, such that, as our life-energy moves along, it flows into these, and takes certain forms quite apart from our present intentions. It is similar to memory, which brings out its old ideas while we are thinking something new. "Habit" would be a good translation for this, as far as it goes, but it does not go far enough. Habit, anyhow, is not very well understood. It is merely found to be a fact in body and mind, and is accepted as such. The old Hindus had their own way of approaching this problem. They held that the past, or "what has gone," is as real as the present, but "in a different way." That being so, the mold created in the past and still existing in its own different way, can operate upon the present, and indeed must do so if there is to be time-causality. This was not considered to be made more understandable by positing a finer kind of body or world in which these molds could be thought to inhere. "A different way of reality" meant just what it said. This way, though not known by our ordinary limited senses, could nevertheless become known to the yogī, who would then become aware of past occurrences.

I will not leave this topic without reference to the cessation of this wheel of pain. We shall see the cause of pain more clearly as the Sources of Trouble weaken. Having realized that we suffer from ourselves, we shall soon remove the cause of pain, which is the covering of the light. I do want to say here, however, that we must not be foolish or fanatical about all these things. The air and mild sunshine in the garden this morning feel lovely. There is no reason why I should not go out there with my writing block this very moment.

Even if we have pain in the present, and have to face that in some sensible way, we need not expect that our future will be full of pain. Patanjali says:

II, 16. *"Pain which has not yet come is avoidable."*

How? By knowing what is the cause of future pain, and removing that cause. We have learned already that the Sources of Trouble are the cause, and we have in fact started to weaken them by the three practices of yoga in daily life. Among these Sources of Trouble we already know that Ignorance is the basis of all the others. This Ignorance associates the self with the not-self, or causes the junction of the one who sees—the Looker—and the things seen, and mistakenly identifies the self with the body. So, says Patanjali:

II, 17. *"The cause of that avoidable (pain) is the conjunction of the Looker with the things seen."*

This agrees with aphorism 5, which defined Ignorance as regarding the not-self as the self. Compare that and the present aphorism with II, 6, which defines Self-personality as identification of the Looker or seer with the mind or instrument of seeing. Evidently we have three things to deal with here—the Looker, the seen, and, between them, the instrument of seeing."

Now Patanjali will tell us first what the seen is, and then the seer, or Looker.

II, 18. *"The visible (world) consists of things produced and the senses, conducts itself as luminous, moving or fixed, and exists for the sake of experience and fulfillment."*

II, 19. *"The Qualities of Nature have divisions—the specialized, the general, the ideal and the undefinable."*

*II, 20. "The Looker is consciousness only, which, though
pure, sees mental images."*
II, 21. "The essential nature of the seen is for his sake."

I will try to explain these four aphorisms together.

The Looker does not change, but sees all the play of objects, that is, the seen. Their very existence is only for the purpose of being seen by him.[1]

Just as we attend a cinema show, and it is not our own life that is being depicted on the screen and we are not supposed to be altered, developed or evolved by it, but only entertained, yet it is shown only in order to be seen by us, so does the world play on for the self or real man, but he is unchanged by it, unsoiled by it—is, as the text puts it, pure.

Now, all these things are compounded of three elements already mentioned, but here (in II, 19), as being in particular reference to something seen or known, they are described as luminous, moving or fixed. That is how they appear in the objective world. I have already described the three Qualities as matter, energy and natural law. Matter appears to the eye in the form of fixed things; energy as moving things; and law as a principle of constancy and order. We must note that law in Nature and knowledge in man are two aspects of one thing. They fit like glove and hand. Because of natural law, Nature, or the world, is "luminous," that is, is intelligible. If Nature did not exhibit natural order or law, but acted in an irregular and fantastic way, man's intelligence could not operate. Indeed it could never have grown, for it would have been thwarted and thrown off its balance at every turn if on one day fire burned us and water wet us and the next day fire wet us and water burned us, and all things behaved in that irregular fashion. There is a correspondence between mind as in man and law as in Nature. Mind and law are both "luminous."

The word "produced," used to describe natural objects,

---

[1] This means they are karmas. "The whole creation is made of the results of karmas; otherwise it would not exist," says the "Shiva Sanhita" (I, 25).

appears to me very significant. It corresponds to what we express by the word "fact." People ask with regard to some thing spoken of: "Is it a fact?" meaning, "Is it really so in the world?" without for a moment reflecting that the word "fact" originally meant something made or produced. Even the substances out of which all objective things are made are themselves made out of the Qualities. Earth, water, fire, air and ether are called the five great products, and are held to have been produced by the great or universal (collective) mind.

All forms or facts are dependent on mind. In our own lives, although we use organized limbs such as arms and hands, it is with our minds that we really make all the thousands of things we use. A carpenter's thought makes a mental picture of a chair, and his hands obey and follow his thought. Even the body, it is said, is a product in this series. Mind moved matter in certain ways, and this by long habit produced the body, expressing functions and endowed with habitual actions and structures. The body is largely a form of lapsed intelligence, as I have explained in an earlier chapter. The bodies of animal life, vegetable life and mineral life are considered to be products in the same way as the human body. All are products.

It must be understood, of course, that all this producing of facts is a collective affair in which there is an enormous amount of overlapping and joint work on one object. Consider as an example that organized thing which is a large railway station or depot. It is full of little brains which operate its parts, from stationmaster to porters, office staff to cleaners, traffic staff to linesmen. I sit there waiting for a certain train to be called. I feel very insignificant. But I am not nothing at all. I have been to the ticket office and bought my ticket— so much intelligence have I contributed to this seething organism. And I have produced a share of this huge fact by paying for my ticket with money that is supposed to represent some work done somewhere by me or by somebody else for me, and exchanged for a temporary share in the use of a railway station and a train. Such is the nature of "the seen"; indeed, of all of the seen, for we are to assume that "stars sweep and question not," on much the same principle.

All these products are fashioned of the three Qualities (matter, energy and law) functioning always together but in different proportions. Where something looks solid and inert, like a piece of clay, it is held that inertness or "matterness" predominates. At the other end of the scale the mind (which also is within the sphere of the Qualities) is made chiefly of law, though containing some matter and energy also. It manifests law, and imposes law on matter, making and controlling separate forms so that they come within its integrating power. On this account we find two kinds of forms in the world— ordered and not-ordered, for example, a table and a drifting cloud. The latter is not strictly a form. As a shape it does not exhibit law, as does an object made by the mind. It does come about as the result of natural laws, but it is the meeting place of several such operations (temperature, pressure of air, etc.) which are not coordinated for the specific purpose of producing this form.

Patanjali's reference (in II, 19) to four divisions in each of the Qualities safeguards us against considering them only as seen by our limited senses. Matter, for example, can be thought of as (a) in a rock; (b) in its rockness; (c) in the idea of a rock; and (d) in its essential nature not defined as shown in a rock or anything else. This division may be regarded as an unnecessary refinement from the point of view of practical yoga. The point to remember is that all these are in the "seen"; even "law" itself is not the "Looker."

Over against all these facts or pictures that constitute the world, we have the Looker or seer. This is called the real man (*purusha*), sometimes called the soul, but understood to be pure, unsoiled, untouched by the world, with all its law and order, its play of forces and presentation of material forms.

Let me stress here the word "Looker" and refer back to our first chapter, where we were told that when ideas are controlled the Looker or seer is in his own true state (I, 3), but otherwise he has the likeness of those ideas (I, 4). The word for the Looker is the same in I, 3 as here, in II, 20, where it says he is pure consciousness but sees mental images.

How are we to understand this? By remembering that we are trying to think of a metaphysical reality, a metamaterial being, not subject to the limitations of the world of facts and forms. He can "see without eyes" and "hear without ears." Add to this the fact that we cannot deny the possession of voluntary limitations by the unlimited. The unlimited can adopt limitations without being limited by them. We must not conceive the Looker as being aloof, for aloofness implies limitation by material process towards simplicity, and takes us in thought towards an ultimate atom rather than towards a causal principle which has the nature of "wholeness" and holds all in its hand. When Patanjali and his associates say that there are innumerable *purushas*, or souls, we understand that each one has his own independence, but also that the unity of each includes the unity of the whole—that the conception does not include a thought of isolation, implying boundary and exclusion.

And when it is said that the essential nature of the seen is for his, the Looker's, sake, we understand it is to assist his process of will, a faculty or function by which a unit of consciousness can focus the whole of itself on a part of itself, and this not on the assumption that it is subject to time, but is the cause of time, and creates time in the act. We cannot say what the Looker gains by it. We cannot even say that he does gain by it, for gain would be an attribute of limitation. He knows all about it, and we shall know when we remove the covering of the light.

You and I have experience which will lead to fulfillment. This experience is in an objective environment or world showing order (intelligibility or luminousness), motion and fixity (II, 18). With the aid of the objective things we develop our powers of consciousness; we increase our conscious grip and grasp in both quality or sense of reality (grip) and quantity or scope (grasp). One reader can take in a long sentence of many lines which describes something with numerous intricate qualifying clauses, while another can manage only the captions in a picture-strip. We increase our grip by concentration or by bringing all our attention to a point on a simple object. This gives us the greatest sense of vividness or reality or clarity that we can get.

Let me give a practical illustration of this. You are sitting with a friend. You have a red rose in your hand. You hold it forward and say, "Please look at this." After a moment you put the rose behind your back and ask your friend what color it was. He tells you that it was red. You then surprise him with the question: "How red?" He looks puzzled, so you say, "Can you imagine that redness? If so, please do so." He assents to this. You now bring the rose into view again, and say, "Please look at it carefully. Does it look redder than it did before?" With a little surprise he tells you that it does. And henceforward, I venture to say, his consciousness of redness will be better than before, for he has increased his grip in that respect, with the aid of an object.

Next, by looking at the object all over and in every detail we increase our grasp without losing our grip. In the process we develop our mental powers. By forcing themselves on our attention through pleasure or pain, objects in the world compel us to focus upon them, perceive them fully and think about them, and so learn. They have no intrinsic value. They exist for our sake. We have, in fact, made them for our self-education. All things are thus worthy to be received and attended to with great consideration and (may I again coin a new word?) acceptiveness.

This is not merely a matter of special practice. It occurs

normally. A dark green creeper grows over a beam on the porch. How much have I noticed it? Have I passed it by as unimportant? Is it just like what happened in connection with a cup of coffee a few days ago, when my wife said to me, "How did you like that coffee? I got a new kind." "Oh, I am sorry," I replied. "I forgot to notice the taste of it." These things, or karmas, stand there with a vividness of reality that can evoke our strongest, clearest, steadiest consciousness, and we treat them like dirt—only, we ought not to treat dirt like that. Look at that green creeper. Respect it. Dwell upon it. Join your mind and heart with it. Let it be with you and in you, and you in it. There will be experience, and great joy. But do not begin thinking, "I am doing this for joy," or "I am now enjoying joy," for that would stop the creeper from doing its work for you.

Thus does the seen give experience and fulfillment to us who are apparently in process of growth. I say "apparently," because if we are the real Looker it cannot be fundamentally so. Is this difficult to understand? Not if we remember that everything depends upon the whole for its very existence, and every idea also. In the apparent growth, therefore, there is no real increase but only a revelation to us of more of the whole of knowledge in the part of the knowledge which—while we are under the influence of the Sources of Trouble—we take to be ourselves. There is not really an increase in our power of consciousness, that is, grip and grasp. But there is apparent increase, which, however, is only a reduction of the covering of the light.

I have a little more to say about the dependence of parts on whole in the realms of (1) things and (2) ideas. This is only to show the principle, from which we can each work out any detail to suit ourselves.

First, things. A book rests on the table. It is where it is because of the table. The table stands on the flooring boards. Those rest on beams, and those on walls and those on the foundations of the house, which rest upon the earth. The earth is maintained in its position in space by the pull upon it of the sun and other globes of the solar system in relation to its own momentum. The solar system is similarly held in position in its relation to certain distant stars, and so on. Even if we say there is a blank between galaxies in which no forces such as we know operate at all, we must say that within the whole that we can conceive everything depends upon the whole, that is, that there is one enveloping causality without which nothing can be what or where it is. "Not a sparrow falls to the ground" without that "father."

Secondly, ideas. We know what any thing is by comparing it with other things. A house, for example, means something to us. If I ask what, you will probably reply, "Oh, a building to live in." This idea has generality (a building), and particularity (to live in), that is, it has a resemblance to other buildings and it has a difference from buildings in general. "My house," you may say, "is the house with the red door." Or, "It is the house on the northwest corner of First Street and Washington Avenue." In this case, house has become general, and the red door or the situation the particular. Both the general and the particular are needed in the statement in which you convey a clear idea of the house to me.

Human knowledge is knowledge of the particular in relation to other particulars. It oversteps the one fact. To be brief: I know my house best by comparison with other houses and other things. If I say: "My house is a sort of box"—that is true, and illuminating. A monkey might say: "A house is a sort of hollow artificial tree which humans live inside of; how funny!" That is also illuminating—it throws more light on my house-idea. In short, the more other things I compare the house with, the nearer perfection is my idea of the house. If I could compare it with all things (and all at once) my idea would be perfect, but in the meantime I have only a personal and incomplete point of view. Hence I say knowledge depends on the whole. In all teaching and learning we attach something to something, not something to nothing in the mind.

Let me pursue this topic once more with reference to motion. I am on the train going from Detroit to Chicago, which is west of Detroit, and I am walking through several coaches to the dining car, which is in the rear of the train. If asked, I would say that I am walking eastward. But the train is moving westward faster than I am walking eastward. So I am really going westward backward at perhaps fifty miles an hour. But the earth is turning eastward "to meet the sun," at that latitude at, let us say, seven hundred miles an hour. So I am after all moving eastward at perhaps six hundred and fifty miles an hour. But the point on the surface of the earth is moving in a curved line, so really I am also rising or sinking (no one knows which!) about nine inches per running mile. The surface of the earth forms an arc, however, so I am going up a bit against the going down, or I am going upper in addition to the upness I am already going. But wait—the earth is flying along in an orbit round the sun (another eighteen miles per second, and in a curve, at that), and the sun with all its satellites round something else, and so on. So, whether I am going this way or that way, or am on my head or my heels, or am only spinning like a top, only Dr. Einstein can say—and perhaps not even he! But this I know, that my real condition of motion or rest derives what reality it has from the whole. Every part depends upon the whole. The whole is not "made up of parts." For the sake of sanity I must now remember "my world." "A poor thing," you may say, "but mine own." And not unlovable. And not without its window into infinity, as we shall see in the next chapter.

Now we come to a group of aphorisms which will not require much explanation, after the considerations we have already entertained. They indicate that quantity is unimportant, and should never awe us or govern our thinking.

II, 22. "Although destroyed for him who has finished his purpose, it is not destroyed, because of the community of others."

Suppose I have finished my work, that is, have reached the fulfillment already mentioned; my Sources of Trouble and my karmas have all gone and I am living in the light and unobstructed freedom of the real self; "my world" ceases, but not "the world." The world carries on for all the other people who still have Sources of Trouble and karmas. Notice here that Patanjali has a normal view of the reality of the world. It is made of karmas due to Sources of Trouble, but it is real. Before this destruction, however, there is "my world"; there is the power or operation of owning and being owned, and the recognition or acceptance of this situation for oneself in the conjunction of the seer and the seen. On this Patanjali says:

II, 23. "It is conjunction that causes the acceptance for oneself of the powers of ownership and being owned."
II, 24. "Of this, Ignorance is the cause."
II, 25. "When that is absent, conjunction is absent; that abandonment is independence for the Looker."
II, 26. "The means to the abandonment is unwavering Discrimination-knowledge."
II, 27. "His wisdom in the last stage is sevenfold."

It is sevenfold inasmuch as it has seven kinds of objects to decide upon—four outside the mind and three within. These will come up naturally in the course of advanced meditation and will represent the following detachments: "I need no more objects"; "I am emotionally attached to no objects"; "I perceive the nature of my independence"; and "I have no more duties."

CHAPTER 7

ABSTINENCES AND OBSERVANCES

I assume that the candidate for yoga has been practicing Body-conditioning, Self-study and Attentiveness to God for some time—at least until they have become fairly easy for him, and he likes them. If he is doing these three things simply because he is "training" or "conditioning" himself for a task, and he does not enjoy them but is glad to drop them frequently, he is not ready to go on to the further yoga practices.

I hope, however, that by now he has also weakened considerably his Sources of Trouble and is ready to enter upon the serious systematic meditations of the man who has "ascended to yoga." He will then start to develop and use the regular eight limbs of yoga.

Let him not think that the limbs of yoga are the branches, as it were, of a tree up which he is climbing. They are his own yoga limbs, with which he pulls himself up, and they remain with him, for yoga is in himself, not in the world. He is to be like one of the pictured or sculptured deities with many arms. He is to become the eight-armed yogī. I imagine myself looking at a photograph of him eating his breakfast or pottering in his garden or talking to his wife, and trying to see whether those eight limbs are there or not.

The light of wisdom that we have been theorizing about in the previous chapter will now be brought to the full point of Discrimination between the real and the unreal. This Discrimination will be in the yogī in character, not merely in thought and memory. As a good man rushes without hesitation into a burning house to rescue a baby, so will the yogī gradually come in this grade to act with Discrimination in all circumstances. His eight arms will help him to this state of being poised in Discrimination.

With these preliminary remarks, I will turn to Patanjali:

II, 28. *"The light of wisdom goes up to the Discrimination-knowledge when there is destruction of impurity through the performance of the limbs of yoga."*

II, 29. *"There are eight limbs, which are Abstinences, Observances, Seat, Breath-control, Withdrawal, Concentration, Meditation, and Contemplation."*

Let us first notice that these eight limbs of yoga fall into three groups:

Ethical—Abstinence and Observance
Bodily—Seat, Breath-control and Withdrawal
Mental—Concentration, Meditation and Contemplation

Patanjali is fond of fives, or else Nature runs in fives. We have had five groups of ideas in the mind. Now in our ethical group we have two fives:

II, 30. *"Of these (eight), the Abstinences are non-injury, non-lying, non-theft, non-sensuality, and non-greed."*

Non-injury, say the Hindus, is the highest duty. The yogīs generally say that non-injury is the basis of all the other Abstinences. Thus they at once put all five of them upon an ethical ground. We must make our peace with society to this extent at the very beginning.

This is an arm of yoga never to be forgotten, so that when you sit down and compose yourself for meditation you must first reflect whether you are at peace with the world, for if you are not you cannot expect your meditation to lead to true intuition. The logic of this is obvious, for any unpeace there may be is due to too strong a Source of Trouble of yours, and the troop of Sources of Trouble begins with Ignorance, as we have already seen.

If now you read all the other Abstinences in the light of non-injury,[1] you will see that non-lying is regarded as for the benefit of others; so also non-theft, non-sensuality and non-

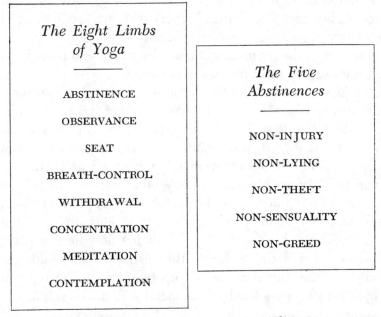

The Eight Limbs of Yoga

ABSTINENCE

OBSERVANCE

SEAT

BREATH-CONTROL

WITHDRAWAL

CONCENTRATION

MEDITATION

CONTEMPLATION

Chart 5

The Five Abstinences

NON-INJURY

NON-LYING

NON-THEFT

NON-SENSUALITY

NON-GREED

Chart 6

greed. Generally the fourth of these Abstinences is taken to refer to sexual continence only, but logic requires a wider connotation. Continence itself needs further remark. The Hindu ideal is that sex-power should be used only when children are desired by both parties. Indeed, the lesson of all this is to use faculties only with their natural intention—speech for the imparting of information, the hands for taking only what is socially rightly one's own, sex-powers to produce chil-

[1] I have translated all five with "non-" for the sake of uniformity of expression and idea.

dren when desired, and possession-power only for what is reasonably necessary to maintain our personality in its functional groove in society, and reasonable comfort, relaxation and education. Somebody asks with reference to the last: "What about old age?" The answer is that we then still have a function in society, for as we associate and converse with people of our social group and others we impart something of our knowledge and character to them.

There is in the proposal of these Abstinences no thought of self-immolation or suppression of pleasure. The placing of non-injury at the head of the group has personal significance, in that it assumes that we are living a life of our own. It adjures us to live that life with as little injury to others as we can, consistent with the maintenance of our own personal utility. It is not thought of as merely negative by the Hindus. I can think of no literature in any other nation which is so fraught with injunctions to the performance of public service, and no other country where such traditions are so often quoted. The rich man is forever thinking how he can plant shade trees and dig wells by the roadside and build rest houses for the traveler, and set up temples for the religion which is in his eyes the basis of social welfare as well as the inspiration of the individual. Non-injury is a safeguard, being an Abstinence, not a rule of life, for living is taken for granted. Whatever your personal personality-life chosen by you and lived with others may be, let it be as little injurious as you can, though it may not be entirely non-injurious till you reach the very threshold of the fulfillment of your life.

II, 31. "Abstinence is a great vow for all occasions and not exempted by life-condition, place, time or circumstances."

For illustration, consider the following. A fisherman may say, "I will injure only fish." Or a soldier may say, "I will not commit murder, but I will kill in battle." These have reference to life-state. I am going to give my own opinion here, which is that the maintenance of one's personality-life in an occupation that involves some injury may be justified by good done thereby in some other direction, which would not otherwise be done. Every man ought to be the keeper of his own conscience. My question for all would be: "Are *you* at peace with the world?" We have in Hindu literature the classic example of King Janaka, who did all that a king should do and yet is cited as one of the greatest examples of success in yoga.

With reference to place and time, someone may say: "I will not injure anybody in church or on a Sunday." He may say that he has not sufficient goodness or self-control to extend his abstinence from injury beyond this place and time. Conscience or no conscience, I think this man is not ready for yoga. But I will put in another category the man who says, with reference to a particular circumstance, "I will not injure, unless it is to protect women and children," or something like that. If the ship is sinking at sea, and some man starts pushing women and children aside to get into the lifeboat himself, I will not hesitate to knock him down, and throw him overboard if need be. It will not be a pleasure, but it will not prevent me from being at peace with the world. It is not entirely casuistry, in fact, if I hold that I have done that man a benefit, not an injury.

The ways of conduct and duty are very subtle, and could not be prescribed for all occasions even in a book of ten thousand pages. In the conflict of duties which we all have to face until we reach fulfillment, each person must decide what to hold and what to put aside on each occasion. Each yogī will come as near to the whole good as he can with reference to all the five Abstinences.

We need examine only briefly the self-regarding aspects of the five Abstinences. Not only non-injury to oneself, but all the other four as well, cover all things harmful to the body. Untruth to others is bound to result in the clouding of our own vision. Every untruth also clutters the mind. "The liar," said someone, "needs a good memory." He has an internal strain, because he has to fit together in memory things which have not lain together in life. The thief: he lives among things which must constantly hurt his feelings, if he has any love in his nature at all. As to continence: the waste of energy involved in incontinence is well known, and the use of that energy in sublimated form in mental work is a thing that yogīs often refer to in their teaching. Greediness in anything, whether the collector's habit or just plain sense-indulgence, injures by cluttering up the body with fat and the material surroundings with things that come back at their owner and constantly disturb his meditations. It also implies dependence on externals for entertainment and a lack of the enjoyment of reflection upon the experiences already gained. To indulge in any of these is to increase their power. The test in this is not that of quantity of things owned, but their organic unity and consequent simplicity of control. This I must say, however, that collections for the promotion of artistry or education or legitimate entertainment and relaxation do not come under this adverse criticism.

The teachers of yoga also emphasize thought in connection with these five Abstinences. One must stop oneself from injuring in thought, and from untruth, stealing, sensuality and greed in thought as well as in deed. We cannot abstain from the acts and indulge in imagination of them, and also follow the path of yoga.

I have spoken of personality-life. This is the place in which to explain that a little more, in relation to self-indulgence. There is a golden mean in the use of sense-pleasures. They are there to tempt the mineral-man into life-function. They are enjoyments for the vegetable-man, and he is apt to overdo them. Animal-man errs by dwelling upon them in imagination and planning to get more of them, and even to revive them when they have become dulled through overuse, by such devices as the spicing of food.

Man-man, however, not only recognizes law and order and proportion and appropriateness in these matters, but he likes the law and loves to live by it. He will reach some perfection of balance in these matters. There is no reason why he should not have nice-tasting toothpaste and sweet-scented shaving soap, as long as these flavors and scents do no harm to the purpose involved.

To others, our personality may be a boon if it is natural to us, and not a pose for the sake of "catching" them in some way, which later, if not sooner, is seen through and instills a little poisonous suspiciousness into social relations. The young ladies dress up; they like it and we like it when it is done to please us, not to impress. It does us good to see good things. It is said in India that to see someone carrying a jar of water is very auspicious; and it does make us happy on the instant. There are some old ladies I know who do me a lot of good by merely existing on the edge of "my world." Men too; I meet them and take something away. Personality is our most precious possession in the world, especially when we not only have it but impress it upon our clothing and our rooms. But pose is hideous, and the pose for others in false and white-washed biographies with which we are frequently mentally fed is one of the worst poison-spots in modern literature. Truth in personality will not hurt in ordinary life. In yoga it is essential. In that, there cannot be pretense, for oneself or others.

One thing more I have to say about this personality. It is considerably marked out for us by our karma. Influences of heredity and childhood years are so great on our personality that they often mark our type throughout life. In general, therefore, it may be well to accept the type, and aim to make it good of its kind. There is yoga in this if the man within lives according to the living laws of the inner self—"to live, to love, to think." God-man may be carpenter or king.

Patanjali next lists the five Observances:

II, 32. "The Observances are Cleanliness, Contentment, Body-conditioning, Self-study and Attentiveness to God."

Cleanliness hardly requires comment; but Contentment is a subject much discussed among students of yoga. It is often described as being satisfied with one's lot in life. I think of it as accepting things and people as they are, and not wishing them to be different. Positive living without wishing is the touchstone of this virtue. Wishing is fatal to yoga, inasmuch as it is an acknowledgment of our own inability. "I wish I could move that mountain; I wish it would stop raining; I wish I had a better house"—what useless thoughts, what waste of time and energy, and how devitalizing! "I will walk round or over the mountain; I will stay indoors and work or write or read; I will make use of and improve on what I have" —these are better thoughts. The truth is that what is, is, and in some way it is for the best; at least we can use our opportunities.

On the other hand, Contentment is not resignation. Even the simplest yogī may say to himself, "I want the shade of a tree," and he will move towards the tree. To be without wants would be to be completely dead. Having formulated our want, we may proceed to act, using what material we can get. The architect and builder know the properties of materials; they do not sit by the roadside and weep because stone is not transparent, or glass will not bend like rubber. They do not *wish;* they *will.*

Contentment is still more than that. It is appreciation of common things. Clay is as good as gold. An enemy is in reality as useful as a friend. Emerson said something to the effect that to the saint, the philosopher and the sage, all days are holy, all things are beneficial and all men are divine. I will not trouble to find the exact quotation; only the idea matters. I admire that contentment of the Hindu villager who values his plot of land, open air, green trees, sunshine and cloud, and room to stretch his eyes above all that he could buy with money earned by spending his days in a factory; and I am happy to see that the new Indian statecraft is largely based on this thought of the true values and proportions of life, and on the desire to secure these goods to the common man. I

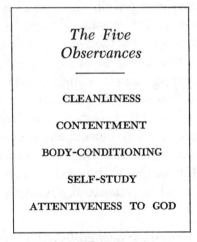

The Five Observances

CLEANLINESS

CONTENTMENT

BODY-CONDITIONING

SELF-STUDY

ATTENTIVENESS TO GOD

Chart 7

think that India may teach the world a great lesson in these matters if she can pursue her ideals without molestation.

Patanjali now brings in Body-conditioning, Self-study and Attentiveness to God over again. They were the whole yoga practice for the novice. But they are also useful to the very end of the road.

The teacher goes on now to tell what must be done if thoughts contrary to the Abstinences and the Observances rise in our minds.

II, 33. *"When there is annoyance by bad thoughts, let there be reflection to the contrary."*

II, 34. "Reflection to the contrary is: 'The bad thought of injury, et cetera, whether done, caused to be done, or approved, whether preceded by greed, anger or infatuation, whether mild, medium or strong, results in endless pain and error.' "

Their results have but to be reflected upon to turn one against them. Nobody really enjoys injuring, lying, theft, et cetera. They are urged on to these because of greed, anger or infatuation. Seneca put it well when he said that the thief does not want to steal, but he wants the article very badly and cannot get it any other way, though he would prefer to do so. As I have before remarked, we are clean within, and to see these things in their ugliness is enough to make us shun them.

We come now to a series of statements about the consequences of perfect achievement of the five Abstinences, which at first glance look like specimens of what is sometimes called oriental exaggeration. In the light of the karma theory, however, perfection of the Abstinences and Observances may very well be believed to produce the results which Patanjali lists as follows:

II, 35. "When non-injury is accomplished, there will be abandonment of animosity in his presence."

II, 36. "When non-lying is accomplished, the results of actions become subservient to him."

II, 37. "When non-theft is accomplished, all jewels approach him."

II, 38. "When non-sensuality is accomplished, vigor is obtained."

II, 39. "When non-greed is accomplished, there arises perception of the method of births."

This man could perhaps get the lion and the lamb to lie down together, did he so wish! The point is that if non-injury is established by spontaneous universal love, there is a force of love which is irresistible. While stating the perfection, the teacher is thinking that in some degree love and the karma of love will be operating in the life of the yogī, will preserve him from at least certain injuries and in some measure over-flow from him to reduce the violence or quantity of animosity in his vicinity. But the yogī cannot be working for that, as even that motive would vitiate the purity of the love. These are by-products that Patanjali is now describing.

Next we come to the power of truth. It is truth in thought and truthfulness in action. The thought and word of one man are as effective as action in another. His mental picture can sway material things in the scope of his world. It is with such an idea in mind that the villager seeks the benediction and fears the curse of the "holy man." This, too, is effective in de-grees, whereby some people have to be careful what they wish, for it tends to come about. The yogī in the complexity of modern life has a task here.

Thirdly, when the yogī is free from the least envy, jealousy and cupidity with regard to things, and more, has a will that other people should have them, and a delight in seeing others enjoy them, the things he needs will seek him out according to the purity of his personality-life.

The next accomplishment is not regarded as merely vigor in the body but as occult power of various kinds, particularly the imparting of knowledge of yoga to others, with or without their awareness of it. There is an idea of "occult children," that is, pupils in connection with this.

The last implies that when we are free from clinging even to the body, our understanding of the processes of life and the lessons of experience will be clear and clean. The eye will be single and the mind full of light.

Patanjali plays quite a different tune when he turns to the perfection of the five Observances. It becomes clear that there are not just ten commandments divided into two groups for mental convenience; but that there are two quite different sets, of which the first is especially world-regarding, and the second especially self-regarding. "At peace with my world" comes to have reference to both inside and outside the body. An old proverb speaks of the saintly man as full of the true self inside and out, like a pot dipped in the sea. The effects of the second five are in character rather than in the outer world. The following are the teacher's statements:

II, 40. "*From (external) cleanliness arises protectiveness[1] of the body and detachment from others.*"

II, 41. "*And then, when there is Mind-cleanliness, come (in order) high-mindedness, attentiveness (or one-pointedness), mastery of the senses, and fitness for vision of the self.*"

II, 42. "*From Contentment comes the obtaining of the highest form of pleasure.*"

II, 43. "*From Body-conditioning, with the decline of impurity, come the powers of the body and the senses.*"

II, 44. "*From Self-study arises contact with the desired divinity.*"

II, 45. "*From Attentiveness to God comes the power of contemplation.*"

In Chapter 4 I have already described the last three and their effects at considerable length. In regard to the effect of Contentment, we must distinguish between pleasure and the happiness or bliss of full attainment. Here we are promised the greatest possible personal pleasure. It will be natural, will it not, when we take delight in everything we have?

[1] The word in the original here comes from a root which means, according to context, "to protect" or "to censure or despise." I have chosen the former rendering, as it accords with practice. It would be strange indeed that dislike of the body should arise from the habit of cleanliness. Desire to protect it from dirt and "bad living magnetism" is much more logical. I knew one yogī who had built for himself in a garden a room of bars appearing not unlike a cage at a zoo, in the middle of which he used to sit, so that when visitors came—some of whom would have undesirable emanations—they would be kept at a little distance. The general view on this matter is that a yogī must be careful of "living influence" in the early stages, but that this is not necessary later on.

I am tempted to tell here briefly about a blind yogī whom I knew well in India for a considerable time. He had no money, but lived in a little cottage which had been built for him on a bare piece of land by some villagers who lived near by, and quite often he went out on visits to people in the country and towns and villages for several miles around. I have never seen a more continuously happy man. When I once spoke to him about his blindness and poverty, he told me he did not mind them at all. In fact, he particularly valued them, because, he said, they had indirectly softened his nature, in response to the kindness of the poor people, working villagers, in the neighborhood. "I am glad of this karma because of the love that has come out of it," he said. "Without it, I might have gone on into future lives still as a hard man." This venerable gentleman showed me that he was endowed with several psychic powers. Among these he mentioned his ability to remember past lives. He told me that he knew in this way that he had been a hard and cruel man when he lived in Delhi long ago.

CHAPTER 8

SITTING, BREATHING AND WITHDRAWING

Everything proliferates in India. The yoga modes of sitting did so long, long ago. Eighty-four different ways of sitting on the ground are well recognized in India. Generally, four of these are preferred for meditation, and it is customary for a person to select one of them for that purpose and keep to it.

Outside this small group, and some variants of them, the postures are regarded simply as health exercises, beneficial in general if properly selected and practiced, and beneficial indirectly for yoga purposes inasmuch as they conduce to an obedient, quiet and healthy habit of body. Some few are taught for bringing pressure on nerves and groups of nerves which are used to develop psychic powers, but these matters are out of place in a course of Rāja Yoga, which does not approve of them.

Patanjali does not recommend any particular posture, but he prescribes a habit of sitting steadily, and gives his reasons for this in three aphorisms, as follows:

II, 46. *"Sitting is to be steady and pleasurable."*
II, 47. *"(This is done) by loosening of effort and thinking on the Endless."*
II, 48. *"Thence there is no disturbance from the pairs of opposites."*

The second of these aphorisms indicates that Patanjali does not expect the student to attain a satisfactory posture immediately. It involves a little effort at first, but gradually there will be less effort, until there is relaxation of attention and the posture can take care of itself. It is not to be assumed that any sitting posture can be maintained without muscular effort, but this can become muscular habit in course of time, like our ordinary muscular habit of holding the chest up and the shoulders square, when walking or standing. That involves some muscular development. Suppose, for example, the student has carelessly become round-shouldered and contracted his chest. It will be advisable for him now to practice holding his shoulders back and his chest up until the muscles will hold that position habitually and without aching—first for a short period and then for a longer period. Apart from the muscles, the joints may be stiff, and this will present a difficulty to anyone who wants to adopt a posture of sitting on the ground as the Hindus do.

I am writing this book primarily for Americans, so need not advise sitting on the ground. You can sit for your meditation on a chair and rest your arms on the arms of the chair, thus relieving the shoulders of the weight of your arms. Then, for the sake of good breathing, I advise stuffing a cushion in the small of the back to keep it upright. In that position you should then see that the head is well balanced on the neck. Perhaps the neck muscles will need a little daily exercise as well as the chest.

Practice your chosen seat now and then, and do not expect to be without some muscular aches in the beginning. At first you may hold the chosen position for two or three minutes, then for five minutes, and so on. To those who prefer not to support the back at all and yet do not find the balance easy at first, I would suggest sitting on a stool or bench or upright chair, resting the arms on a table at first and later on on the thighs fairly close to the body. Ladies will often have to obtain a low chair or stool, or wear high heels, because it is a bad thing to let the front edge of the chair press on the underside of the thighs behind the knees. Ordinary chairs are made for men. They are too high even for people 5 feet 6 inches tall, which is above the average height for women in North America.

The above instructions are for those who want to sit up rather formally to do their meditations. But I would say from my own experience and that of others that it is not at all necessary. Meditation can be done lying down or reclining in a deep chair. Only, let the chest not be compressed nor the spine bent. The objection to lying down is that it conduces to sleep, by mental habit, whereas meditation requires the maximum of mental alertness, the opposite of sleep.

Among the Hindu postures is one called "corpse-posture." It is often prescribed by their old-fashioned physical culturists to be done after violent exercise, and is described as giving exquisite pleasure. They spread a mat on the ground and lie down flat on the back upon it, with the arms along the sides and without a pillow. Then they relax, beginning with the toes, and proceeding little by little up the legs, trunk and arms, to the neck, face, eyes, ears, forehead and even the scalp. They do this for about fifteen minutes, thinking upon something pleasing—a tree, a picture, a person, anything. Then they get up immediately refreshed.

When you have learned to use this posture for relaxation without a tendency to sleep, you can use it also for meditation instead of an upright posture if you wish. This can be done with the arms at the side or with clasped hands supporting the head. Or you can lie on a couch, with a sloping upper part. The requirement is that there shall be no strain in the body, and no cramping of the lungs. A special warning is needed with regard to strain, for sometimes people, when trying to meditate, tense the muscles of the neck and arms, clench the teeth and draw the brow into a frown, and then get headaches and similar troubles. This will not do. The body must be at ease.

Still, I must say something more about sitting on the ground, because more and more are people liking to sit on the beach or in the garden, and sometimes there to practice a little meditation. The method of sitting with the legs crossed in various ways is really difficult for Americans and Western people generally. Our legs are generally thicker and stiffer than the legs of the Hindus. But there is a form of what is called "the pleasure-posture," in which a scarf is used, which is very easy. You sit down cross-legged, with the knees moderately raised, pass a long scarf round the small of the back and tie it round the knees in front to support their weight. Then rest the hands with palms together on the cloth in the valley between the knees. In this position hands, legs and back are all well supported, and there is easy loosening of effort and no cramp, even after a long time.

A variety of this posture is to clasp the knees with the arms instead of with a cloth; and another variant is to clasp only one leg with the arms and let the other leg rest sideways on the ground with the heel near the groin. The old Rajput soldiers used to sit with one leg up in this way, instead of with the legs crossed on the ground, so as to be alert and ready when required for action.

I must explain what is meant by "no disturbance from the' pairs of opposites." The idea is that the world assails us constantly with opposites calling for adaptation on our part. Heat and cold, pleasure and pain, moisture and dryness, light and darkness, quiet and noise—all the extremes are trying to us, and they generally distract our attention. In meditation, however, we want to forget the body for the time being. When it is settled in a comfortable posture we can do this, as, when there is no exertion, changes of temperature are least likely to affect it; and to meet them, processes of breathing and perspiration automatically take place. Yogīs who intend to meditate for long periods go further, and select a place sheltered from wind and sun, "not too high and not too low, not too large and not too small."

One more piece of practical advice. When you sit down to

meditate, remember the principle of non-abruptness. Quietly and gently dispose the body into its intended posture, and equally quietly take gentle leave of your current thought-subjects, turn the mind to what you are now doing for the body, and just imagine that it is to be quiet, without intention to move, like the quietness of the "Endless." The Hindus have an image for this—the picture of a serpent lying coiled up, a serpent named Endless, on which God, as Vishnu the preserver, is pictured as taking rest during the sleeping-time of the worlds. To think upon this induces in their minds the strongest and clearest conception of restfulness, and this mood they then apply to the body.

Western people instinctively put on a mood for swimming, or a mood for lifting a weight, or a mood for work and all the rest, which moods prepare the body for the intended purpose —and yet they hardly realize that they do so. Hindus, with their vast study of psychological processes over thousands of years, with knowledge which has become practically hereditary in their bodies, have developed a great science of moods in connection with what the West often thoughtlessly assumes to be ignorant worship of images and pictures. While we are in meditation, the body is to be our Endless.

Next Patanjali gives us five aphorisms relating to breathing. When our thoughts are quiet, our breathing is quiet and steady. Observe the slow and steady breathing of a sleeping person. When we wake up and begin to exert the body, that breathing is disturbed. If we lift a weight we instinctively fill the lungs and hold the breath. In that case the mind really causes the change. Merely to think of lifting the weight with intention to do so tends to produce the same effect, because of the habit of thinking in connection with action. But, quite obviously, thinking and meditation do not require this change of breath, though the bodily action would. When there is concentration of mind, there is a tendency to disturbance of the regular breathing, to such an extent that sometimes the breath is unconsciously held up until there is a sudden choking.

For good meditation we therefore need to tell our breathing to go on regularly and quietly. We need a steady habit of breathing just as much as a quiet seating of the body. Otherwise, disturbances in breathing will react and spoil the meditation. Patanjali tells us to compose the breathing to some regular measure, but leaves it to each one to find the measure that suits himself. The aim is to stop the mutual disturbances of function of mind and breath. He says:

II, 49. "When that exists,[1] *regulation of breath is the next consideration. It is control of the manner of movement of inbreathing and outbreathing."*

II, 50. "The condition of the breath as outgoing, incoming or standing still, is regulated as to place, time and number, and becomes lengthy and fine."

There are certain schools of thought and practice of a form of yoga which is called Hatha Yoga, which prescribe, among other things, the influencing of mind through various methods of abnormal breathing. For this there is a set of technical terms, among which are *pūraka,* the inward movement of the air into the lungs; *kumbhaka,* the holding of the air in the lungs; and *rechaka,* the outward movement of the air from the lungs. A practice of breath-control recommended by these schools is as follows:

Preparatory exercise: Close the right nostril with the right thumb; perform slow inbreathing (*pūraka*); perform slow outbreathing (*rechaka*); repeat several times; remove the thumb and close the left nostril with the right third and fourth fingers; perform inbreathing and outbreathing several times as before.

Prānāyāma proper (regulation of breath): Close the right nostril with the right thumb; perform slow inbreathing; close

---

[1] When the sitting is steady and pleasurable.

the left nostril with the right third and fourth fingers; perform *kumbhaka* (i.e. keep the breath standing a while in the lungs); remove the thumb and perform slow outbreathing; perform slow inbreathing; replace the thumb; perform retention (*kumbhaka*); remove the fingers; perform slow outbreathing. This process constitutes one *prāṇāyāma* of the Hatha Yoga system. You are now at the beginning, and can repeat the process the number of times desired.

This practice is dangerous except in very strict moderation. It is usually carried on with the timing of one unit for inbreathing, four units for retention of breath, and two units for outbreathing. The unit may be a measure of time at choice, perhaps two seconds in the beginning. It is usual to lengthen very gradually both the unit and the number of repetitions. In regular working of this method, a unit of about four seconds would be short, of eight seconds long.

I have been told by medical men that the average person, when quiet, takes about twelve to twenty complete breaths in and out in a minute. The time differs very much with different persons. Twenty per minute would, I think, imply rather shallow breathing. For meditation, much slower and deeper breathing is better. The question of the amount of oxygenation of the blood that is needed during meditation, and whether any appreciable time is required for the chemical process, has not been gone into, I think, by modern scientists, so length of breathing still goes by rule of thumb. I have found about six breaths per minute a fair time-rate for meditation in most cases, but each person should experiment to discover what suits him best, in accordance with the natural releases due to accumulation of carbon dioxide and the absorption of oxygen.[1]

---

[1] There is a certain calmness of mind which reflects itself in rather slow measured breathing. The more excitable an animal is the quicker is the breathing. A hen is more excitable than a duck; it breathes about 30 times per minute to the duck's 20. A monkey breathes about 30 times per minute, a dog about 28, a cat about 24 and a horse about 16. A slow breather is the tortoise, with only 3 per minute.

In Hatha Yoga schools it is held that the practice of using the nostrils alternately has a special effect upon the nervous system. Patanjali makes no mention at all of the practice. He does not even use the terms, *pūraka, kumbhaka* and *rechaka.* I have given these technical terms in order to say and emphasize that Patanjali does not even refer to them. He uses the untechnical terms of ordinary speech in referring to inbreathing and outbreathing. He says that *prānāyāma* is the control of the movements or gait of these two. He says that the outward, the inward and the standing conditions of the breath are to be supervised as to place, time and number, with a view to slowness, and fineness or delicacy. In brief, the breathing is to be the reverse of excited or noisy.

I have described the Hatha Yoga form of breathing exercise because it is often taken for granted that Patanjali intends that. I wish to refute that idea and to say that, in fact, this holding of the hand to the nostrils would disturb and spoil the meditations which Patanjali has in view. He does not want the triple form of *prānāyāma.* So he goes on:

II, 51. "A fourth (condition arises) which casts aside the business of external and internal (breathing)."

This appears to me simply to mean that after a little practice, or even mere carefulness, a condition of breathing arises in which you need not think of breathing, or of place, time and number for it. The breath falls automatically into the right mode for meditation. It ceases to be an object of attention. In fact, such state is necessary for successful meditation. You cease attending to it, just as you forget your seat. And then:

II, 52. "In consequence, the covering of the light is diminished."
II, 53. "And there is fitness of the mind for Concentration."

After this disposal of body and breath, the covering of the

light, or karma in the shape of bodily interference, is diminished.

Read aphorisms II, 51-53 as one continuous statement, and it becomes clear that Patanjali wants merely good breathing, not something abnormal with which to affect the mind from the outside. Body action of any kind as an aid to meditation is foreign to Rāja Yoga.

We come now to the fifth limb of yoga: withdrawal of the senses. Patanjali's aphorisms on this subject are two, as follows:

II, 54. "There is withdrawal of the senses, when they are detached from their own proper business and are imitating, as it were, the nature of the mind."

II, 55. "From that comes complete obedience of the senses."

In Hindu philosophy senses are something different from sense-organs. So they are in real life. The sense-organs may be alive and well, in perfect condition to transmit messages from the outer world to the consciousness within, but sometimes that transmission is not performed. With the eyes open, we sometimes do not see; with the ears open, we do not hear; and with the nerve-endings in the skin in touch with material objects, we do not feel anything there.

The reason for this is that impressions from the sense-organs become sensations only with the active cooperation of the consciousness within. Light waves of the red range, for example, only announce their presence by a sensation of redness when there is at least some attention given to them. So withdrawal is a fact. We now learn that it can be voluntary.

Withdrawal is not only possible; it is so common as to be constant. We are never aware of all that the sense-organs are sending in. The power of attention is selective and cannot deal with a large variety of things at one time. While reading a portion of this book you have probably not noticed that there is a sensation of pressure—a kind of touch—where you are in contact with your chair. Perhaps you have not noticed the sound of an airplane which is buzzing overhead, or the calls of the birds outside the window. Perhaps you have been so interested that you have not noticed that someone has been in the room and has spoken to you without effect, and seeing you "absorbed," has kindly withdrawn.

Patanjali considers that you should deal with this external phenomenon—external to your consciousness—as you have dealt with the world, the body and the breath, in the Abstinences and Observances, Sitting and Breathing, which we have studied earlier in this and the previous chapter. Being at peace with the world, we can forget it during our Meditation; next the body and the breathing are both to be peaceful.

As we settle to our Meditation we first give thought to those things. Have the children had their supper and are they all right? Yes: well then, off with them to bed. And so with the senses. We have to say to ourselves that we are going to give our mental attention to some chosen subject for a certain definite or indefinite length of time, and then tell the senses that we have no business with their objects for the time being. We may know that certain noises are likely—cars passing in the street, or someone turning on the water in a room near by, or a dog barking. We can now review their likeliness and announce that we are not going to be interested in them for the time being.

Thus we can train the senses not to worry us; and they do, in fact, conform to what is in our minds, for in our meditations we can have all the color and sound and other sense impressions we may want for the time being.

The senses do accept a sort of instruction, and, if we wish it, they go further and work for us without bothering us. They will inform us of certain things if we wish it. We can give the instruction, "Hear nothing else, but tell me if the doorbell rings," and this will be done, in much the same way as you can tell the senses to wake you at a certain time. I found in this connection that when my watch was wrong they woke me by the wrong time of the watch, not by that bigger watch that has wheels made of the earth and sun!

An interesting case within my knowledge is that of a friend of mine whose wife frequently suffers from some form of heart trouble. They have twin beds in their bedroom, not side by side, but in separate corners. Their apartment is in a town on a busy street where cars go by early and late. He is blessed with good health and the habit of sleeping like a top. But at the least restless movement of his wife at any time of the night he is awake on the instant, and up to see what he can do. Remembering such cases as this, we can practice the art of withdrawal, until we can easily slip into that condition which Pataniali describes as complete obedience of the senses.

CHAPTER 9

CONCENTRATION, MEDITATION AND CONTEMPLATION

At the beginning of his Book III, Patanjali explains the last three limbs of yoga. These are called internal, because the work of yoga is now within the mind itself. It will be remembered that the first two were connected with life in the outer world and the next three with body, breath and senses. These three internal limbs complete the set of eight.

These last three limbs are correctly translated and exactly described by the words Concentration, Meditation and Contemplation. Patanjali says:

III, 1. *"Concentration is the binding of the mind to one place."*
III, 2. *"Meditation is continued mental effort there."*
III, 3. *"Contemplation is the same when there is the shining of the mere object alone, as if devoid of one's own form."*

It is now appropriate for us to describe the method and object of these three acts.

Concentration

Concentration is giving the full attention of the mind to any one thing or idea. Looked at externally, it is a narrowing of the field of attention, but internally it is focusing one's mental power.

Normally we pay attention to everything within range, without focusing very definitely on any particular one. As we sit in the theater before the curtain goes up, we take in the general view of the stage, curtain and framing, the wall and ceiling decorations, the lights and the people in front of us, but when the play opens we forget most of these things and concentrate on the players, and, among them, on the central group. Similarly, Mr. Wilkins, the entomologist, going along a country lane, is suddenly deaf and blind to all the rural sounds and sights when he becomes interested in some little creature an eighth of an inch long sitting on a tiny leaf.

Once more Patanjali is asking us to do at will something that we commonly do spontaneously, when he proposes the practice of Concentration.

There are two aspects of this matter. One is length of time —when we deliberately concentrate on some chosen subject or object for a more or less lengthy period. The other is decisiveness—that ability for swift and full Concentration which is expressed when we turn to observe an object or think of an idea. The latter ability is largely the result of the former practice, and when it is well developed we have our maximum consciousness of the object of our attention, which is then very well lighted up. We have gained by our practice a better quality of consciousness, a greater vividness of mental life.

People differ greatly in their degree of awareness or mental awakening to life and things; that means also in their appreciation of reality. We must note that this is one of the most important things in life, in which it is very evident that a man's future depends upon himself—upon his own self-cultivation. Nearly all success in life depends upon concentration, quite apart from any interest in yoga.

People say that it is quite easy for them to bring their attention to a point on one thing or idea, but it is difficult to keep it there. A person has decided to concentrate on, let us say, a rose; after a few minutes he suddenly awakes from a daydream about a concert to which he has recently been, or an imaginary conversation with some business associates, to realize that he has forgotten all about the rose. He brings his mind back to the task and very soon the same thing happens again—and again. Fortunately, I can help him to put a stop to that trouble, by means of what I have called the method of recall.

First of all, a few hints. When you concentrate mentally on an object, let it be in its natural setting. The rose will perhaps be thought of as standing in a vase on a table. If you picture the rose as merely floating in the air somewhere in front of your eyes, you will have at least a faint sense of holding it there. In Concentration, you should not hold the idea. You should just place it in its proper setting and then look at it. After you have made the imaginary picture of the cut rose in the vase standing on the table you can close in your attention upon the rose alone, without its adjuncts, saying to yourself that your interest is there.

Remember that your objects should be so natural in thought that moving things seem to be moving and still things appear impressively still. Dancers must dance, singers sing, and flags flutter in the breeze.

My second hint is that you should merely *look* at the rose in your imagination, as quietly as possible. Some people get quite tense in their efforts to concentrate, and thereby give themselves bad headaches. It is really injurious to the body to concentrate with tenseness. The object of our previous practice of easy seat and calm breathing was to relieve the body of tenseness. In this matter it is the same. Look quietly at your object, just as quietly as you would look at the clock to see the time, as quietly as you would hold a feather in your hand. No effort is needed to look, and no effort of any kind should be made when concentrating.

We come now to the practice of recall. Put your rose in place, look at it mentally, and then think of everything else that you can—one thing after another, not all at once—without losing sight of the rose. Other thoughts will be there, all around, but your original thought will still be in the center of attention. You will begin, perhaps, with "roses I have known."

That will be quite a fruitful source of many thoughts. You will next, perhaps, think of roses of different colors and different kinds, and then of other kinds of flowers to some extent resembling the rose, or growing in proximity to roses you have known. You may go into detail about the rose, and look at its petals and other parts, and, not confining your thought to what is seen, think of its scent also, and try to smell that mentally just as you try with mental sight to see the rose. You will, perhaps, think of some of the natural associations of the rose —the bush on which it grows, the path beside which a bush you know may stand, the florist's shop where roses are displayed, and even the Rose Parade at Pasadena. You may go further afield and think of the rose in literature, and history, and symbolism, or still further to rosy clouds, and rosy hopes. But—this is vital—*all* without losing sight of the original rose.

Now, what does this mental effort do? It produces a mental habit or mood of returning. Ordinarily the mind wanders on from one idea to another, as I have said before, and this mode of following the path of least resistance is the mental habit of most people, who therefore find that the wandering continues even when they try to concentrate. It will now be observed that the practice of recall induces exactly the opposite reaction. Every time that you send the mind in search of another new thought about the rose you do so with the intention of keeping the original rose well in view. Thus is induced the habit of returning to the center. There is a mood connected with this. When you put on the mood of Concentration the mind soon begins automatically to return to the center from every other thought that may arise.

After practicing this method of recall a little time every day, or on odd occasions perhaps in bus or train, you will find it easy to keep your thought on one thing for quite a long time without any trouble or fatigue at all. If you do find yourself tired after Concentration, do not fail to look into the matter and find out what is wrong. There is some tension somewhere, which ought not to be. What is wanted is attention without tension.

I must mention another matter which often gives trouble—disturbing thoughts due to emotions. Generally these intrusions are from troubles in actual life; somebody has spoken ill of you to someone else whose opinion of you is important; or somebody has passed disparaging remarks about your new hat. These troubles are sometimes very serious ones, such as unemployment, family worries and ill health. The emotional habits connected with all these are such as hurt pride, anger, despondency or fear—at least these are the commonest. Such things being, they may very easily come up and disturb your Concentration on the rose.

Without doubt, the best way to deal with these disturbing elements is to give them their due, and think them out. Do not try to drive them out or beat them down. Often people worry, and try a hundred times to drive out the worrying thought that spoils their sleep, their work and their meditations. But back it comes, every time.

If you find such a thought disturbing your Concentration, decide that you will think it out. You need not stop your practice in order to carry this out immediately. Treat the thought as a semi-human thing—there is a bit of our life in our thoughts so that the mind is full of little devils and angels of our own begetting. Speak to it and say, "Please don't trouble me now. I promise you at least half an hour's interview this afternoon at three o'clock"—or whenever it may be—"and we will go into the trouble fully then."

Keep the appointment, play fair with your mind, or you will soon find more complex troubles there. When the time comes, sit down and think over the whole matter of the trouble in all its aspects. Examine every detail. In other words, think it out and leave no loose ends. You really need not make any vital decision, for it will decide itself—if any action or inaction is involved—when it has been completely examined.

If, however, there is only a decision involved such as whether you will go to the country or the sea for your vacation, and you have considered all the pros and cons in the matter and yet you are still undecided—you may as well toss a coin to settle the matter, for if pros and cons are about equal it does not matter which way you decide. If you feel you need more data for decision, go after the data. If you are not able to get the data at present, make this decision—that you will leave the matter undecided until such and such data come. Do not worry about what is not in your power, but settle fully what is.

There is another thing that you can do if persistent thoughts of the nature of repetitive fatigue-impressions or other almost mechanical things keep breaking in on your practice of Concentration. I am thinking now of things that do not arouse hurt pride, anger, fear, depression, etc. When you see them coming around near your rose, just say to them, "Oh, you are there again, are you? Well, I don't care. Stay if you like; go if you like. I am interested in the rose, and I do not mind if you come into the room as long as you do not expect me to pay particular attention to you, so as to remove the thought of the rose from the center of my view." Thus treated, they will slip away when you are not looking. You cannot drive them away, or watch them go away, because in so driving and so watching you will be transferring your attention from the rose to them. This is similar to the fact that you cannot watch yourself going to sleep.

It is a good plan at the beginning of every practice of Concentration to settle yourself in quietly and gently—let there be no abruptness ever in these practices, be it remembered—and say to yourself, "Now I am going to look at a rose, and I am not interested in anything else in the world during the next ten minutes. There is, in fact, no reason why I should be interested in anything else, because there is plenty of time for everything else in the rest of the day. Now, on with the rose."

Remember, too, this other side of Concentration; during the day, whenever you have something definite to do or to think about, give it your full attention, so that you feel at your best. This increases your observation and your sense of reality. Waking, exercising, bathing, dressing, eating, drinking, talking, walking—be fully awake to what you are doing and look every fact and thought straight in the eye.

Sometimes people ask whether they should or should not concentrate upon parts of the body or centers in the body. To concentrate upon a toe or a fingernail or the tip of your nose does no harm—any object will do.

In general, I would say, do not concentrate *on* your heart, or stomach or nerve-ganglia such as the solar plexus, because you may by your thought disturb their natural automatic functioning. If you concentrate *in* them—that is quite another matter. The position of Concentration is of psychological interest. Most of us lead such a life of sight—the use of the eyes takes such precedence of every other sense—that when we sit to concentrate we think of ourselves as being somewhere inside the head just behind the eyes and looking forward to an object which then is placed, as it were, in front of the face at a convenient distance for sight.

If our object is one that appeals to our sense of smell, we almost instinctively "put ourselves in the nose." In the case of hearing, this process is more obvious. Do we not sometimes close our eyes and feel ourselves in one or the other ear when we are intently trying to identify a sound coming from an unseen source? It is a good practice to be in the nose to smell the rose, to be in the hand to feel the touch of it, and to be in the eye-center to see it, and it would be good to be in the ear to hear it if it were a thing that made a sound.

People sometimes ask whether they should or should not concentrate on abstract ideas as well as concrete things. There is no objection to this. I would say, use simple things in the beginning, then more complex ones, then abstract ideas. Ideals, virtues and personages are subjects more for Meditation than Concentration. Another matter: it makes no difference in Concentration whether you "see" or "visualize" the object or not. You may just think of it.

Meditation

Meditation is a continuous and complete flow of thought with reference to the object of Concentration. It is Concentration continued with a difference. Having centered your attention upon the rose, you are now going to think all that you can about it, so as to know it as fully as possible.

This sounds something like a repetition of the practice of recall already described. There is this difference—Concentration involves contraction; Meditation, expansion. In Concentration you were sending your thoughts away to one thing after another while keeping your attention at home, but now you are adding thought to thought to complete your picture or your mental grasp of the rose.

Meditation is not different from proper thinking, but it is the opposite of mind-wandering or dreaming or sleeping. In it you are not only observing the rose and its parts and qualities and functions, but also the relatedness of all these particulars, a full knowledge of which can make your rose a unitary thing. This is just like a piece of artistic work, which is a kind of visible meditation, wherein our statue or picture or poem or even novel must be a unitary thing if it is to be good.

In such a unitary thing or thought two features are to be noticed—naturalness and logic. Naturalness has reference to sense-experiences in the world; logic to the relationship of the functions of things, or in other words to the syllogistic structure of the world and its parts in their time and space relations.

It is naturalness to picture a pen in a hand in the act of writing, or even a pen clipped in a pocket or awaiting use upon a desk, for this is common in experience, but it would violate the principle of unity if we were to try to picture a snowman eating a fountain pen. It is natural to think of a motor car as going on wheels, but I defy you to picture with any success such a car as walking or running on legs and feet. Much of new art violates this unity. It may be instructive in depicting the condition of the junk-shop mind, but in this case it instructs in what not to do and how not to live, as does the science of psychiatrics. But I will say this for it also, that on occasions it has reference to a unity beyond the present scope of the average observer.

The Meditation that Patanjali is interested in is the yoga-Meditation. There are plenty of other meditations, which are for a purpose, such as meditations on virtues for the sake of building character, or on ideals for providing guiding stars in the course of life's journey. But Patanjali's Meditation is only intended as a stepping-stone to something beyond ordinary perceptions and utilities, or even glorified anticipations in their categories. For the moment we shall have to call his aims intuition and ecstasy.

To the Hindu philosophers, the human mind with all its thought has never appeared to be an instrument of truth. It is only an extra or indirect sense, and it has the groping character of all the senses. In yoga we are to go beyond thought, and to know things not in their juxtapositions but in their relations to primal unity.

As I said before, the animal-man develops a mental cunning, which is hardly to be called understanding, but is compounded of a collection of knowledges about the nature and logical relationships of things. A university man who had several degrees once told me that he felt he had "no brains," as he expressed it, but only "a sort of low cunning"; I admired him for his perspicuity, yet I could see that his knowledge of himself at least contained something more than low cunning. The forest lore of the animal and the society lore of the ani-

mal-man are an extension of that simple mental deductive-
ness which tells us that when a shadow appears there is a
corresponding object round the corner. Much of our most
valuable science is but a prodigious extension of this faculty
of indirect sense-perception. It does not inform us as to what
things really are. Fortunately we do not need that information, for all our life and the good things connected with
material living and the enrichment and improvement of character and social relations are on the surface or near to it. We
need not wear our coats inside out, with all the seams showing.

This rather involved preamble of mine to the subject of
Meditation may confuse the reader. He will ask: "Why, then,
should Patanjali propose that I think fully about the rose?"
The answer is that at the end of full thinking lies the gateway
of intuition. It is not by going back to the mental condition
of the cattle grazing in the fields that we shall attain human
perfection, but by going forward to complete thought about
what comes through the senses into our minds.

Now to the practice, as I would prescribe it. Sit down, review your peace with the world, attend to seat, breath and
senses, concentrate on the rose and begin your Meditation
as follows. What do I know about a rose (1) for sight—shape,
size, color, of whole and of parts; (2) for sense of smell; (3)
for sense of touch; (4) for mind—its class (flowers) and
comparison with other members of that class, its cultivation,
what it expresses? In short, think everything relevant that
you can that will help to complete your picture of the rose.

At the end of such a Meditation you will have done two
very good things for the mind. You will have coordinated or
unified many ideas which were previously lying confused and
unconnected in the mind, and you will have awakened in the
mind a set of inquiries, where your knowledge was lacking.

It will partly explain this if I mention here a piece of advice
about reading and study which I have often given to my stu-

dents. It is to read to correct and supplement your existing knowledge. You know what subject you are going to read about on a given occasion. Review it before you open your book. Bring out all the thoughts you can about it, however few they may be. Do not be satisfied with a cursory glance at the subject. Wring out all you know or can think of. After all this, with all your previous knowledge revived and co-ordinated and with mental hunger in the form of questions, open your book and read. Finally close the book again and mentally review what you have learned. Review it occasionally for several days. New knowledge is like little plants, which need to be watered occasionally while they are young.

The thinking process in Meditation should not contain repetitions. Sometimes people perform repetitions of a word to blot out unwanted thoughts. When they are angry they will repeat, "Love, love, love . . ." or when they are hurt or despondent they will repeat, "Happy, happy, happy . . ." It produces an effect, but the seeds and causes of anger and despondency remain and will sprout again. Or those who wish to "build in a virtue" will chant over and over, "Kindness, kindness, kindness . . ." or "Courage, courage, courage . . ." The proper way, however, to deal with these things is to meditate with full thought upon pictures or examples of various acts of kindness and courage—to look at them from every point of view, to sift from them every bit of dross or pretense or secondary motive, and thus to get as near as possible to the emotion-core meaning of these things. For they are essentially realities of character, not particular kinds of action in certain specific events.

There is, however, one word the repetition of which Patanjali permits and even enjoins in his course of yoga. It is OM, which we have already studied in Chapter 3. Repetition of it is enjoined because it is regarded not really as a word but as a sound-symbol for the free life, and thus a focal point for meditation, as the rose was focal in our present example. In this instruction there is room for that expansion of the object which is characteristic of meditation, in contrast to the contraction of the object which is the first feature of concentration.

It is interesting to notice that in our thinking there is something analogous to the beating of the heart in the body—contraction and expansion follow each other with regularity in the process of learning. We concentrate on a subject to the exclusion of other things, and then we expand that subject in what we call study and thought. In the expansion we make the complex simple—at first there are unrelated facts which make a complex collection, but afterward they have fallen into their places in one organic or unitary mechanism, and there is now a simple idea or piece of knowledge, in which they all have their place—the miscellaneous building materials have become a house, the wheels and pivots and catches and springs have become a clock. Blessed is that human life in which there has been so much real thinking or meditation that there remains nothing scattered about, but the whole mind is simple and redolent of unity.

Similar to the Meditation on ideals and virtues is the Meditation on personages. If this is done not for purposes of yoga, but for the building of one's own personality, no one can say that it is a bad thing. If the girls copy the ways and appearances of the film idols of the moment, we perhaps can expect an elevation of the social structure in certain particulars. But suppose these youngsters meditate upon those examples and steal the life out of them, they will soon thereby think the form to death. What began in copying will through Meditation continue in understanding and fructify in creative and original thought. The bee has sucked the honey from the flower, and the bee departs on its own business.

There was a tradition in some occult circles that when the pupil reached the highest initiation he had to kill his teacher. The meaning is simple—the Master is not the form that appears and speaks words. In nine cases out of ten that form is created by the pupil even when the words speak truth. The Master in the pupil thus speaks to himself. And inasmuch as the pupil has to come to the life, he must perform that meditation in which the form vanishes and the life alone shines forth. Akin to this is the tradition that the personality of a Master is an illusion.

So also in the end of our Meditation upon the rose: in the fullness of thought it will be seen that this was only a window into the infinite.

We hear of Meditation on the real self. This cannot be, inasmuch as in the psychological process the ultimate subject and object can never be the same. That is why such Meditation must always be characterized by negative thinking. "I am not my fingers and toes, my arms and legs, my shoulders and hips, my body, my thoughts, my feelings or even my will." This will not release us. We must know what those things are, not what they are not, to find the self. Affirmations, whether positive or negative, only attach one thing to another. "More radiant than the sun and purer than the snow is the self within me." Radiance? Purity? Attachment again, and covering of the light. Light? There is no way of escape within the mind, though the captive pace up and down forever.

So Patanjali prescribes control, not drift; and fulfillment of object in transcendence of thought.

Contemplation

It will help to an understanding of the nature of Contemplation if we remember that there is a shuttle action between object and consciousness. By attending closely to an object, we obtain our keenest experience of reality. It is at the same time an experience of ourselves.

Lying on my writing desk is a teapot lid. The teapot has long since been broken. I have kept the lid here because of its exquisite pattern. I have long admired the beauty of it, but just now I took it up and looked at it afresh—very closely. I realized that I have not seen it properly before. It fills me with immortal delight. At the moment I can believe the maxim that art alone endures.

Someone will say: "You see a beauty which is not there. The cat and the dog do not see it." I answer: "I see a beauty which is there. I do not see it when I merely sit with my eyes shut."

My companion says: "You merely sit on your own dunghill and crow with pleasure, because you are born of the dunghill and its nectar is in your blood." I answer: "No, for with proper attention I see that beauty everywhere. And yes, to this extent, that I belong therefore to the whole of things."

It is true. If I now concentrate my attention on one little piece of the pattern of my teapot lid and meditate upon it, I get that same filling with the beauty-light, and I can say truthfully to myself that I am willing to live for this, and indeed this is life. We are all willing to live life. It is a living tomb that we abhor, and there is delight when we discover that the catacomb is of our own making, and that the mind which made it was not essentially at fault but entered this tunnel to come out some day at the other end.

Yes, I look at one tiny piece of the pattern. It is something like the edge of a leaf. There meet only two lines and a bit of color, but with this Meditation they become my window into infinity. This beauty is life of which I can never tire. Oh, I have lost myself in life, and found myself in its beauty!

That beauty belongs to the whole, the whole that is the maker and upholder of all parts and is revealed in the smallest of them as much as in the largest. Beauty, like truth and love, is of the whole, and in Contemplation we receive its revelation, and our own self-becoming.

With this knowledge, it becomes clear that in Meditation and Contemplation we have the fulfillment of faculty, not its dissolution, and the reception of revelation. This is not to be achieved by reduction of mind on a backward path to animal-man and vegetable-man and mineral-man. Contemplation is a kind of worship, reached through a Meditation in which we value experience, and a Concentration which grips the things of sense with the hand of a brother.

The senses give us the norm of reality—let us never lose sight of that iron fact. When I look at the green leaves of the tree outside my window, some gray stones built into a little retaining wall holding flowers—beds with blooms blue and yellow and red—and I see behind those some portions of the white walls and red-brown roof of a garage, and near to me on a table some money and a key and a pair of scissors and two or three opened letters, when also I hear the singing of the birds and the ticking of my clock, and I feel the floor beneath my feet, and the seat beneath me, and a little movement of air against my cheek—I know that I am at my best among these things and that through the senses I have my best reality and my best being. I have known this a long time. What I had to learn was that the smallest of these was of equal quality with the greatest, and equally a window to the infinite. I rejoice to know that my fulfillment of life is to be also a fulfillment of things and events and the common scene, so that at last there will be nothing to decry or shun.

The practice of Contemplation is simple. All you have to do is to complete your meditation on the rose or other chosen object. When you have brought out all your knowledge and ideas about the rose and done all the thinking that you can about it, consider whether you are seeing it from every point of view or only from one position. You must see it not merely from the side, but also from all sides, from above and below, and from its own center.

When you have thought all you can, do not leave it, but poise your consciousness at that point—poised at the height of your meditation, very still, but fully awake, keeping the full reality of your sensuous vision, looking at the object from within. Now a moment will come when new light will be revealed—call it intuition, some effect in the brain whereby it becomes aware of what it could not catch before. Intuition dawns, or sometimes flashes, and with it the ecstasy that means more life.

May I descend to a common example of such emergence or revelation in ordinary experience? A chemist mixes together hydrogen and oxygen—two colorless gases—and passes a spark through them. At once, "they combine to form water." But wait a minute—let us be more exact in our observation and our language. What do we see and know? They combine, and water appears—water, which bears no resemblance to either hydrogen or oxygen. Water appears. Water is something real, is it not? I prefer to say that water is manifest. This combination reveals or embodies water, not makes it.

Another example. The daughter of my friend plays a melody on the piano, note after note. If she played the same notes separately, one at five o'clock, another at ten minutes past, and so on, there would be no melody. But the association of those notes in a mind that has time-grasp, reveals the melody. Music is not in the notes which embody it; it is revealed.

So in Contemplation comes the revelation which we call intuition. Something new in Nature but having the permanence or timelessness of all reality is there manifest in a space of time, and is born in our consciousness. At its lowest, contemplation so disposes the brain cells that they have a new awareness, a new admission of reality.

We have manifestations of involuntary contemplation in every department of inquiry. Archimedes wrestled with the problem of how to discover whether or not the golden crown had been tampered with by the substitution of an alloy for the original gold. He did all the thinking he could and at last, in his bath, the solution jumped into his mind, and he jumped out of the bath and ran into the street shouting "Eureka, eureka! I have found it, I have found it!" Many another scientist, artist, musician, philosopher, devotee and poet has done the same thing in his own way.

I think that we have herein the secret of that greatest bugbear of the evolution theory—how can the future come out of the past, the complex out of the simple, the organized out of the unorganized, the brain and heart of man from the primeval mud? I think the answer is that it does not, but that there is a progressive revelation or manifestation in our darkness of some new aspect of the infinite reality, and that all evolution is emergent and not at all creative.

This thought agrees with yoga experience and it also solves the problem of illusion raised by the old Hindus, who found out that things are not what they seem and yet they instruct us. They said that things, though false, lead us to reality, just as in a dream the imaginary bite of an unreal snake can awaken us from the dream. All is clear with the analogy of the use of a rag doll by a little girl. We are seeing ourselves in the so-called things.

Experience and the use of faculty—in the shuttling of these two extremes life finds itself and its perennial fulfillment. Common sense and impulse are found to be reliable when seen in the light of this knowledge. The popular insistence on fact and events is sound. Writing and reading are poor substitutes for conversation and vision. The telephone is preferable to the letter—not because of its speed, but because in the use of it life is nearer the fact and further from the symbol.

That rose—we have now lost our personal angle. We are conscious of it, as a young child is conscious before it has developed an idea of its own personality—with the full vividness and reality of experience. This happens in Contemplation, though we cannot make it happen and cannot watch it happen. It is as Patanjali says: "There is the shining of the mere object alone, as if devoid of one's own form." As if we were not there. But we are entranced. Intuition comes, and with it ecstasy.

This explains why it is impossible to enter into Contemplation with personal intentions. If you want intuition you must be willing to accept what comes without wishing or hoping for anything in particular. This is where faith comes in. And faithfulness, too; for the intuition must be obeyed, or the power to receive it again is lost by the intrusion of self-personality.

Review now the three stages through which we have come —in Concentration we focus on something; in Meditation we get our best view of it and carry to the highest point of our thought the life-quality or clear consciousness of experience; and in Contemplation, poised there, we become the receptacle of more of ourselves—more being, more consciousness, more happiness, which is experienced, not pictured in thought.

CHAPTER 10

THE MIND-POISE

After describing Concentration, Meditation and Contemplation, Patanjali again turns from practice to theory. All along the way he wishes the student not merely to perform certain practices, but also to understand why. The practices would produce their results without the knowledge, just as in walking it is not necessary for us to know the ways in which the leg and foot muscles operate; but in this case, as something new is being done, a knowledge of the process helps to warn the student away from misapplications of the purpose.

Patanjali wishes to allude often to the three inner limbs of yoga, so he gives us one name for the process, as operating in succession as one unit. This is in accord with practice, as we always begin with Concentration and pass through Meditation to Contemplation. He says:

III, 4. "The three, in oneness, are Mind-poise."

Oneness here means one continuous operation. The three are successively applied to one object. This term "Mind-poise" describes the condition of the mind in relation to the object of contemplation. The mind is to be perfectly poised on the object. There is an implication of restraint only in the fact that the student is holding himself back or away from something else while holding or poising the mind in all its positivity. This positivity will appear clearly in our next chapter, wherein I give Patanjali's numerous statements about the effects of poising the mind on certain specified things.

Sometimes the idea of trance has been attached to the

third part of this Mind-poise. But the word Contemplation presents the correct idea, for the word trance generally implies that the person concerned has become physically unconscious. The intention here is quite the reverse. The yogī's brain is in the highest condition of alertness. Yet we could speak of him as "entranced," inasmuch as he is rapt away from things other than the object of his Mind-poise. We may be entranced by the beauty of a scene, but we would then be most awake or alive, not scatterbrained, but poised on the beautiful scene. All the powers of the mind are gathered together in agreement (*samādhi*) on the one thing. Even in our involuntary contemplation of a beautiful scene, we find that this is exactly what happens.

Comparing these three limbs of yoga with the five earlier ones, Patanjali says:

III, 7. "*The three are more within than the preceding ones.*"

The ablative case—the word "than" here—indicates relativity. This is important. We must know that we are still not really "within." The wording here guards the student against the mistake and danger of being satisfied with the achievement of poise upon any particular thing.[1]

The real inner is, of course, the very central self beyond mind. That is why Contemplation is described as of two kinds —the Contemplation with cognition and the Contemplation without cognition. The difference between these two is the subject matter of the most advanced part of the yoga course. I will write something about it further on. At present, I will

---

[1] In yoga you must not define your goal on any occasion, unless it be when you say that you wish to find the real self, in which case you also remind yourself that you do not know and cannot think what that is, and that even the word "self" is misleading. You are aware, indeed, that it does not come into any category, cannot answer to "what," and is only for temporary convenience referred to by noun or verb. I have already mentioned that one must never predetermine in wish or in idea what is being expected in intuition. To define a goal is correct procedure when you are making something objective. So let the student not think of the achievement of Contemplation on anything as his real inner and final aim or effort.

merely allude to the triple source of the mind's seeking for knowledge. It looks "downward" through the senses at all objective things—that is, at all things which are spoken of as "it." Secondly, it looks "level" at other minds or persons, whether human or not—that is, at all coming within the category "you." Thirdly, it looks "upward" to the unitary monitor within—to that which it is able to call "I" after it has by careful thought pushed the body (an "it") and all personalities (those of others and its own—which are all properly "yous") out of their frequent roll of masquerading as "I."

I must here allude to another school of philosophy, the Vedanta, particularly the non-dual (*advaita*) philosophy of Shankarāchārya. In writing about that school I have elsewhere emphasized the teacher's practice of lumping together all the "its" and "yous" and calling them all "yous." Knowledge of things or persons in these two categories is all knowledge of the objective, but that cannot be said of the "I," if the "I" knows itself. That would be direct knowledge. All other knowledge is also, in the last analysis, knowledge of the self, but it is indirect, through its use of "its" and "yous." It is thus convenient and psychologically accurate for Shankarāchārya to lump all the "its" and "yous" together in one class, for when trying to understand the distinction between self and not-self we can then simply say that all "yous" (including my own "you") are outer or objective.

This explanation makes it clear, I hope, why Patanjali says of the three elements (Concentration, Meditation and Contemplation) of Mind-poise that they are only "inner" or "more within" with reference to the previously mentioned five limbs of yoga. They are not inmost. The teacher goes on:

III, 8. "*Even that is an outer limb with reference to the seedless.*"

"Even that" means even the poise of Contemplation-with-cognition. The "seedless" is another name for the Contem-

plation-without-cognition. The Contemplation-with-cognition may also be called "Contemplation with seed."

Mind-poise on an object (that is, with cognition) is "with
seed" because the process of Concentration, Meditation and
Contemplation on an object always ends by delivering you
back where you started from. If you start with a rose, you
end with the rose. You end with some intuition or insight or
illumination which you did not possess in the beginning, but
you end at the same point of contact with the world. Your
Mind-poise has produced results and those will lead on to
further results by the ordinary process of thought and action
which is life in the world, and it is therefore "with seed." New
conditions of life in the world will sprout from it.

It is, of course, open to you to say that you want to practice
Contemplation-with-seed for the purpose of improving your
life in the world, and do not want the seedless Contemplation
—at least not yet. There is no objection to such a decision.
It is important that we should be honest with ourselves, and
never pretend at all.

Suppose the question is put to you in some occult manner:
"After you die, at some future time, do you want to return to
birth in this world, assuming that you can have the kind of
body and environment chosen by yourself?" If your answer
is "Yes," or "Not exactly; I want a better world," the Contemplation "with seed" is for you. Really, the Contemplation-
with-seed is for all at the beginning, and it will eventually
lead on to Contemplation-without-seed—but there is no
hurry. Each man's life must ripen in its own way, and he will
know at the proper time when he wants the Contemplation-
without-seed. The decision cannot be made on intellectual
considerations, such as "That is better, or higher, and I ought
to want it and go after it."

When you end a Contemplation, which, as I have explained, delivers you back at the object which was your start-

ing point, your mind will be full of thoughts, and these will have their effects upon you and other people and objects in the world. Among the Hindus it is commonly believed that every thought of man on being conceived sends out its messenger, so to speak, having some influence upon people and things, and further that it also adheres to its creator and works on him, being in some degree a preparation for action, so that he will some day feel the effect and have some result from even his most idle and trifling thought. The seed, they hold, is bound to grow and lead to fruit.

We are now going on with the study of the Contemplation-with-cognition. Patanjali says that it is applied to particular kinds of objects, and the benefit is the attainment of intuition or "cognition-sight." He says:

III, 5. "From mastery of it (i.e. Mind-poise) comes intuition."
III, 6. "Its application is to grounds."

Sometimes we get knowledge by smelling, tasting, touching, or hearing things, sometimes by reason, sometimes by being informed by someone else (a reliable witness, of course), and sometimes we have the inner light of knowledge, illumination or intuition.

I maintain that it is a psychological fact that all cognition is fundamentally intuition, and all knowledge contains a core of the intuitive, by whatever process it may be attained. If we are walking in the country and we see a large object in the distance and then we say to ourselves, "There is a house," we do not immediately see it as a house, but there is a moment between seeing and knowing which is a moment of intuition; then the truth in us recognizes the fact.

Similarly, if a teacher is instructing a class, there is a pause between a student's hearing of his statement and his realization of what it means—a pause of intuition. All the fine arts are well versed in this principle; in their different ways they create the pause which gives us the poise from which intuition arises. Poetry and sculpture most obviously create this pause. Even the putting of a frame round a picture does a good deal, does it not? Even my little "does it not?" does it, does it not?

Now to the question of "grounds." In a meeting or a debate we refer to "the ground of discussion." We expect the speakers to "keep to the point." Elsewhere in these aphorisms (I, 30) we find Patanjali referring to one of the obstacles to successful concentration as missing the point or losing the ground. When Patanjali here speaks of grounds, we should not assume that he is thinking of stages or "planes." He has given no grounds for this. Further, we could not put "missing the stage," but only "missing the point" in translating aphorism I, 30, where the same word is used. Clearly both the wording and the context of our present aphorism (III, 6) indicate that Patanjali is informing us that he is here dealing with the objective or with-seed Mind-poise. That is why, in III, 7, and III, 8, he says it is not the real inner, but is external to the without-cognition or without-seed Contemplation.

Patanjali next proceeds to some further psychological study of the process. He now makes use of the word transformation, or change. The word transformation is best, because it makes us think of the rearrangement of something to present a new form, whereas the word change may lead to less careful thinking, in which we dwell on the idea of an assumed process rather than the concrete facts. The point is that at one moment a thing has a certain appearance, and a moment later a somewhat different appearance. These are its transformations.

We are to study now not the idea which is before the mind, and is the ground of the application of Mind-poise in any given practice, but the condition of the mind at this time. The mind has its transformations or conditions, its changes.

Just as water is sometimes solid (its ice-condition), and sometimes gaseous (its steam condition), so the mind has its transformations or conditions. I have elsewhere called these "moods."

In Chapter 8, when giving instructions on the how of Concentration, I explained the practice of recall, and stated that it gave rise to a mood of recall which automatized the process of concentration. Such a mood is what is here called a transformation or a condition of the mind. I am not laboring the point, except to make sure that we know what we are about— the study of transformation or mood, not of transforming or changing.

That being clear, we have now to consider the function of control. Must we say that when we are performing a Mind-poise we really are thinking of two things—the object and the control? Are we to suppose that the control will be lost (and with it the ground) if we do not keep it also in mind? The answer is: No, because control is not a ground, an idea, but is a mood.

Just as by practice one becomes able to put on a mood of concentration, so by practice also arises the mood of control. This is not different from what occurs in common life in the body. A man is round-shouldered and stooping, and perhaps his doctor says to him: "Hold yourself up, man; square your shoulders, throw out your chest and keep your abdomen in." This man thenceforth pulls himself up every now and then. Walking along the street or sitting at his desk, he will straighten his back and square his shoulders and throw out his chest and draw in his abdomen. And some day he will be pleased to find that this has all become easy, and when he gets up in the morning from his relaxed condition in bed, he puts on the correct mood with a thought so slight that he hardly notices its existence, and now his posture or condition or transformation takes care of itself. When, at some time, this man decides to take a rest by lolling in a deep chair or reclining on a couch, or going to bed, with the slightest thought he changes his mood to one of relaxation.

Someone says: "Oh, that's nothing; that's only habit." Well and good. Call the control-transformation a habit. The slightest thought will press the button and the mechanism of the mind does the rest. The point is that with practice you can establish a control-transformation or mood, so that, having started it, you need not think of control when you are performing Mind-poise on a particular idea or object or ground.

After this preamble we can proceed. Patanjali says:

III, 9. *"The control-mood is the association of the mind with the control-moment, when there is the decline of the habit-mold of mind-spreading and the rise of that of control."*
III, 10. *"By habit-mold there arises a peaceful flow of it."*

I must comment on the use of the word habit-mold, as meaning more than mere habit. The *operation* of the habit-mold is indicated in aphorism III, 9, and that is simply habit. Therefore in aphorism III, 10, we have to think of a training resulting in habit such that the condition becomes easy. This thought runs through all the eight limbs of yoga, as well as in the transformation discussed here. The habit-mold is sometimes alluded to in the simile of a weaver; in the world, the cloth remains even when the weaver goes away; similar to this is what remains in the mind after the attention has been withdrawn.

The words I have translated in III, 9, as rise and decline have a much more combative flavor in the original. One means coming up, emerging, manifesting; and the other means defeat, subjugation, being overpowered. The spreading and the control are thought of as wrestling with each other—at one moment A is on top; at another moment, B.

Patanjali now speaks of the contemplative condition or transformation of the mind. He says:

*III, 11. "When there is the rise of one-pointedness and the
decline of all-interestedness, there is the contemplative
condition of the mind."*

"Rise" means in full force, as when we speak of the rising
of the sun. Without this mood of one-pointedness, Contemplation will fail. We start it with Concentration and carry it
on through Meditation into Contemplation. The habit of recall, which I have fully described in Chapter 9, means that
when there is a decline of one subject of thought there is
immediately a rise of the same, not something else.

Says Patanjali:

*III, 12. "Further than that, when the subsided and arisen
mental images are similar, there is the one-pointedness condition of the mind."*

Here again one could have used the word "mood" instead
of "condition." It is the prevailing mood that causes the re-
arising of the same thought.

The effect of the prevailing mood upon the flow and drift
of thought in ordinary life is not noticed by everybody, yet
it always exists. If we unexpectedly pronounce the word
"pitcher" in the presence of a number of persons, some will
think of a certain kind of vessel for carrying liquids, others
will think of the thrower of the ball in a baseball game, and
these minds will go on flowing—one perhaps, to Rebecca at
the well, and the other to various teams and places, and so on,
according to their respective moods.

We should note, proceeds Patanjali, that it is not only the
mind that has transformations. Every object has them. A
thing is regarded as the carrier or support of properties, at-
tributes or characters. As far as our direct knowledge goes,
the whole world consists of nothing but many properties or
qualities constantly changing. We can see, for example, that
a flatfish is sometimes gray and sometimes brown. We say

the flatfish *has* these qualities. We think of the flatfish as something permanent there amid the changing qualities, but in fact the idea of permanence of an object arises because the qualities do not change all at once. We actually see only a bundle of qualities which present rapid transformations to our view (as when the milk goes sour on a hot night), or slow transformations (as when a little boy grows into an old man).

On this, Patanjali says:

III, 13. *"Similarly are described the transformations, properties, characteristics, and states of objects and senses."*

III, 14. *"The object is the preserver of the characters, whether subsided, risen or still to be named."*

III, 15. *"The change due to succession is the cause of the change of transformations."*

To put the matter of these three aphorisms in simple language, I may say that when we see the flatfish gray at one time and brown a little later, we see gray and brown and several other things, all of which are being replaced by something else, quickly or slowly. These qualities, properties, characteristics and conditions are believed to be held together by the flatfish, and some of them are past or gone, others present, and still others not yet namable because they belong to the future. They cannot manifest all at once, but must do so in succession, and on account of this the object shows transformations.

CHAPTER 11

ON PSYCHIC POWERS

Patanjali presents us with a long list of unusual faculties and powers that can be attained by Mind-poise on various objects. For a long time in the West we have been in the habit of calling these "psychic powers." We are now tending to replace the word "psychic" by "paranormal," as it has the advantage of not prejudging the cause or source of any particular unusual experience, but allows us first to observe and record, and afterward to consider what part is played by mind and what by the body in any particular phenomenon or type of phenomenon.

We long ago divided paranormal activity into two sections: faculties and powers. By faculties, we understood such paranormal perceptions as psychometry, clairvoyance, knowledge of the past and the future, microscopic and telescopic vision, communication with distant persons, reading and entering the minds of others, visions of distant scenes and of Nature in "higher spheres," understanding of the sounds of animals and foreign languages and so on. By powers, we meant paranormal activities such as hypnotic control, abnormal control of bodily functions, levitation, control of "elementals," traveling in the "mind-form," movements of objects without contact, materialization and dematerialization, and healing by touch or at a distance.

These things have been known to the Hindus from the most ancient times. They have been known to most other nations also, in various degrees and forms. America today is full of independent exponents of these arts. Some of the older religions established special departments of augury and prophecy, of healing of bodies and remission of sins, of easy contact with the "gods" or "angels" or the divine, even to the point of transubstantiation and its physical agency of communion, all connected with paranormal faculties or powers. But the Hindus do not set much store by psychic powers. You may travel through a hundred small towns or villages and you will find hardly anyone who, though believing in them, would think of working to obtain these powers.

The people know about these powers, and when a "holy man" happens to come their way and let out some evidence that he has seen past lives or can now see what someone is doing at a distance, they admire and reverence him, but they see that both for his life and their own the paranormal is not the economical. They are ready to accept and even to buy amulets and talismans, and do generally perform various small ceremonies on special occasions to ensure auspicious conditions for the crop that is being sown or the welfare of the new-born son or whatever it may be.

The best clairvoyants I have known—and I was in daily touch with persons having psychic powers for many years—would prefer to open their newspapers and read them, in some cases with spectacles on, to gaining general knowledge by clairvoyance, or trying to get their news from the ether.

There is another thing I have noticed in this matter—that clairvoyance is not as reliable as physical sight. For example, in the case of one whom I had the opportunity to test with scientific care a great many times, for both telepathy and clairvoyance, the results were one hundred per cent correct, insofar as that the object was always named, but still in every experiment a personal modification was introduced without the knowledge that it was such. In one case a simple picture of a hen was transmitted. This came out as a hen in a farm-yard, surrounded by her chickens and scratching the ground to get food for them. The greatest divergence in the same series of experiments, but with a different receiver, was when a table knife transmitted was received as a pocket knife. I noticed in all cases within my experience, except for some Indian yogīs whom I was not in a position to observe for very long, that the personal factor came in. In matters in which there was strong personal interest, this would color and modify the information received, while not destroying its essential character.

The chief cause of the indifference to psychic powers of the Hindu aspirant to yoga is that he regards all of them as within the sphere of things which he is trying to overcome. The things seen by clairvoyance and psychometry are merely more of the same kind of things as are seen by the physical eyes. It is just an increase of the collection of ideas, painful and pleasant, which at present keep him in bondage, and which he now proposes to face and master.

It is not that he aims to escape from them by suppressing or dodging them, as I have already explained, but by Mindpoise on an idea he proposes to master it and thereby fulfill his own strength. It is as though one should decide to become a violinist. One does not need a hundred violins or all the violins in the world. One is enough; it is the practice that matters. The simile is good, for the musician is ultimately going to reveal the music that is within himself. Do not tell me that he is only going to imitate and enjoy some music composed by another man. That is his object at first; he concentrates upon a piece; he meditates upon it until he has it to the full, and he will go on doing that until he really has it to the full, and the same beauty is awakened in himself as found its birth in the original composer; then the floodgates of his own musical soul will open and he will be a master and servant of the heavenly harmonies of the real or archetypal world.

Patanjali brings this subject forward with his usual directness when describing the psychic powers. In aphorism III, 34, he describes two kinds of knowledge, one being experi-

ence through the senses and the other knowledge of the self
or real man. There is a fundamental difference between them,
he says, in that the first kind is "for the sake of another" and
the second "for the sake of itself." We are all aware, I think,
that the knowledge that we call experience exists for others'
purposes, that is, for our purposes. It is not a living reality,
but only a form or idea. It is not a sort of gnome or fairy
which might be imagined as dancing about and singing "I
am knowledge, and I enjoy being myself, and I like becoming
more and more and more!" But knowledge of the self or real
man is to be conceived of as the living knowledge, knowledge
knowing itself to be knowledge and itself. This is only a
groping definition in "words of discovery," of course, and
will be replaced by the yogī, on the fulfillment of his task,
with a realization of self or reality which cannot be known
beforehand. Patanjali says:

III, 34. "*Although the pure mind and the real man are absolutely incognate, experience does not present the idea
of their difference, because it exists for the sake of another.
From Mind-poise with himself as object comes knowledge
of the real man.*"

III, 35. "*From this arise insight, higher hearing, touch, sight,
taste and smell.*"

III, 36. "*These powers in the spreading mind are injurious to
Contemplation.*"

I have already explained that the nature of the mind is to
respond to all things in the category of "it," and to produce,
preserve, alter, arrange, remove and destroy things in that
category. The mind is called spreading because its interest
and activity are surging out, and therefore are opposed to
the process of Contemplation. All things entering the mind
attack our poise and peace, for every one of them is a problem. They stand up there, challenging and questioning, and
until we have understood them, put them in their places and

fitted them into our lives, they are like besiegers. It is the constant trial of the yogī that while he is trying to put his existing mental house into perfect order new experiences keep on coming and they have to be fitted in to form that simplicity in variety which is the manifestation of unity perceived and reflected by the will.

The triple process of Mind-poise, it will have been noticed, involves the gradual gathering together into perfect order, of the fullness of the yogī's past experience. Mastery of the past opens the door to the future, to more light and life. More things, more experience, are just a living death—servitude is death—until they are mastered, that is, unified in the mind and the life.

Imagine then, what happens if an aspirant to yoga becomes interested in what are called the psychic powers. New and far-reaching facts of the world flow in at that wide-open door, new puzzles and problems and duties arise from these and, be it observed, unless he has uncommon will power he will very soon become confused, next faddy, then silly and finally mad. If he is a violinist, dozens of violins of every shape, size and color will poke their noisy faces at him out of every door and window that he passes, when—as I have already said—one violin is enough for the sane man.

I must here philosophize a little on the damnable nature of the lure of material greatness. Sometimes, when I see an enormous crowd of people cheering a crowned head or goggling at a race meet or a ball game, I think: Is it possible that all these people have been born?

I think of the labor, the emotion and the planning that have been expended upon each one of these, and I realize that in those humble endeavors, so poignant and rich, the true greatness of life (which is qualitative, not quantitative) is manifest. The product does not matter in the same direct way. In the living moment the clouds are rent and all heaven is there. It is on such thoughts, not on new powers, that the yogī's

Mind-poise will be rightly expended, and with their aid he will uncover the light.

In his Section III, aphorisms 16 to 33, Patanjali has already listed a number of attainments which can be achieved by Mind-poise. He puts them in their proper and inferior place in relation to the essential purpose of yoga in the aphorisms quoted in this chapter. Having herein studied their nature and effect, and noted that the "powers" are injurious to full Contemplation, let us now look them over.

Supplementary note to Chapter 11.

Emerson has a nice poem, named "The Day's Ration" which illustrates this wisdom of glad acceptance of our small portion of the world, in the perfection of our attention to which we find ourselves possessed of the true quality of our being. It begins:

> "When I was born,
> From all the seas of strength Fate filled a chalice,
> Saying, 'This be thy portion, child; this chalice,
> Less than a lily's, thou shalt daily draw
> From my great arteries. . . . '"

Another reference to this quality appears in the same poet's lines (from "Musketaquid"):

> "The cordial quality of pear or plum
> Ascends as gladly in a single tree
> As in broad orchards. . . ."

These thoughts should release us from the oppressive feeling of being brow-beaten by bigness, which is really only collective-ness, and should show us that in pure things and events, however small, there is for us a windowness into infinity.

CHAPTER 12

SEVENTEEN PSYCHIC POWERS

III, 16. "By Mind-poise upon the triple transformation comes knowledge of past and future."

The triple transformation is a technical term. It means that the changes or transformations which an object undergoes are of three kinds, described as of quality, specific character, and condition or state. We must be careful about our words. I have spoken of changes or transformations, not of changing. In common parlance, we speak of the changes that an object undergoes, and we get thereform an idea that the object is changing. In this matter, however, we think of a succession of transformations—it will therefore be noticed that the conception is concrete throughout, without the introduction of the abstract idea of changing.

As I understand it, the quality of a thing is that which gives it its primary character—for example, a chair, it would have been said by many of the ancients, has the quality of chairness. This chairness is taken to be a reality, manifest in the chair. It will be questioned whether there is any such reality; it is, however, also questionable whether the fact is as commonly believed in our day, namely, that we give personality to objects and that a chair is a chair only for us because we think of some object of a certain shape[1] which is convenient for us to sit upon in such a manner that we support both but-

---

[1] In the terminology of modern physics we might say that the chair is really a certain grouping of force-vortices; but the old Hindus would not admit the total absence of materiality in any sense-object. Those inherent constituents of the chair are, in this view, not pure energy, but energy subject to resistance, the character of matter, which occupies space and resists any other occupancy of the space so occupied.

tocks and back. To a cow, for example, that object would not be thought of as a chair. We ask, then, with regard to a furnished house in which nobody is now living, is that object a house or is it not a house? The ancients contend that it is still a house and that its houseness is a fact. Categories and classes are natural and are facts. In common with all other made things, or facts (the exact meaning of the word "fact" is something made, as before mentioned), this object is a fact, and its chief characteristic is chairness.

With respect to a particular chair, there must be something that distinguishes it, so that we get a definition such as, "the chair which is made of wood, is of such and such dimensions and shape, has a padded seat," etc. etc. This gives us the secondary quality or definition. Thirdly, there is the condition of the chair, new or old, broken or perfect, and so on. I have mentioned these points before, but it is necessary to review them again now, in relation to time sequence.

In course of time an object undergoes transformation in all three respects. We are not permitted vaguely to think, "The chair is getting old; we doubt whether it can be called a chair any more, for certainly no one dare sit on it." If we want to practice Mind-poise on that object for the purpose of knowledge about what has gone—the past—and what is yet to come—the future—we must do it on the transformations, not in the abstract.

This is not the place in which to discuss at length the question as to whether past and future can or cannot be known by what must be called paranormal vision. I would refer those who are interested to the plentiful literature which exists on the subjects of clairvoyance, psychometry and prevision. Patanjali takes it as a fact without question, as all the yogīs do. I have had sufficient personal experience in this field to know that such knowledge is a reality, though by no means common, and quite often imperfect or tainted with ideas already existing in the mind of the percipient. We have already noticed the stress laid by Patanjali on the control of ideas as necessary for successful Mind-poise; it also plays its part in the avoidance of this taint.

III, 17. *"There is confusion of word, object and mental image, because of superimposition upon one another. By Mind-poise upon the distinction (between them) comes understanding of the sounds made by all creatures."*

This means that commonly people do not trouble to distinguish between a word, its conventional meaning or the object to which it is applied, and the idea in their own minds. The principle of yoga is always to apply a meticulous attention to the thing in hand, to avoid confusion. In this case we have to strip away the conventional meaning and our thoughts from a particular sound or word. Human words are conventionally arranged to express and convey ideas, but the sounds of animals (and some sounds made by human beings, such as "O, ah, hee-hee, um," and many others) express feelings and emotions. Even in articulate human speech, intended to convey ideas by conventional meanings attached to the words, there is also tone, expressing emotion, and tonality expressing suppressed or residual or "built-in" emotion.

The purpose of the Mind-poise described in this aphorism is simply, I believe, to understand the mind-counterparts of sound—not articulate and conventional words—made by various beings. The use of the word *ruta* (sounds) in the aphorism indicates this. For articulate alphabetic sounds the word *varna* is used. For sounds produced by other means, such as the sound of a drum or of bamboos rubbing together in the forest, or of a mountain stream, the word *dhvani* is used.

I may mention here that the whole art of psychometry and clairvoyance depends upon contacts. There must be a point to start from. A good psychometrist whom I knew well used to receive numerous letters asking various questions. He would reply, telling the writers to send a small object of contact—a fragment of an article or, in the case of a person, a bit of hair or closely contacted thing, such as a scrap of cloth or a piece of writing. He would say that he could get from the letter as a contact-article to the mind of the writer and thence indirectly to the other person or object under consideration, but this was wasteful of energy. Similarly, in the present case, the yogī must hear the sound; that is his starting point.

III, 18. *"From bringing into consciousness the habit-molds, results knowledge of previous life-conditions."*

The word here translated habit-molds is very difficult to put into English. I have already explained it, but let me do so again, in connection with the present aphorism. The main idea is that every thought and feeling of ours leaves behind it a definite impression somewhere in our being, although it is no longer within our consciousness. This produces various effects, such as habit and memory, and also gives our life always the tendency to flow into old molds in all matters with regard to which our volitional consciousness does not happen to be active at any time. Here lie all the impressions from our past, which go on operating with the life we put into them when we formed them, until they are brought out into the light of volitional consciousness.

According to Patanjali and most of the old thinkers of India, these habit-molds carry over even from previous lives, so, by digging into himself or others the yogī can obtain knowledge about past life-states. I have come across a number of instances of such deliberate "looking up past lives." In one case, an Indian yogī related to me some of his own past lives and some which he told me were mine. One lady I knew in England—who had to some extent proved her psychic powers to me by repeatedly submitting to tests in thought-transference with great accuracy—used frequently to describe other people's former lives. As the details thus told had in the main close reference to their present impulses and interests, this particular example held closely to Patanjali's habit-mold linkage mentioned in the present aphorism. I had also the experience of being present at a research of this kind into nearly fifty previous lives of one person, at the same time involving less closely the past lives of about three hundred other persons, of whom many were known to me. In this case also linkage of the habit-molds was very evident. Quite apart from any judgment of mine as to the probabilities and improbabilities of admixture of the psychic's personal interest and imagination presented in any of these cases, we have here an example of one of the paranormal developments brought out in connection with yoga practice.

III, 19. "(From bringing into consciousness) the mental images (in the minds of others) arises knowledge of other minds."

In this aphorism I have carried over "from bringing into consciousness" from the previous aphorism, as being implied. "Of others" is also implied. We have considered the sounds made by others, and the habit-molds possessed by others, and now we come to their ideas. The yogī will, if he wishes, be able to know the mind of another person. It is generally understood that this means the state of mind—whether there is love, or fear, or pride, or truth, or whatever it may be—but not the object of such thought or feeling, unless that is made the subject of a further definite Mind-poise.

There has been quite a vogue among European and American "psychics" to get this "knowledge of other minds" in an objective rather than a psychological manner through the intermediation of color-vision. The mind is seen as "an aura," and in the aura various colors are seen, which are interpreted to indicate particular states of mind, as for example, a pale, clear yellow for pure intellectual activity, a blue for devotion and a green for sympathy. Whether this is due to the scientific or objective habit-molds of the Western mind, I cannot say.

III, 20. "From Mind-poise on the form of the body, when there is a stoppage of the visibility of it, light and the eye being disconnected, comes the 'internal state.'"

The last word is generally interpreted by my Hindu friends to mean invisibility. That is undoubtedly a very old idea of the meaning of this aphorism. "Invisibility" expresses the matter from the external point of view. The original word emphasizes the withdrawn condition of the yogī. I have not myself witnessed this phenomenon of a physical person becoming invisible, but it is quite commonly talked about and believed in India. This is not the same as the case of a yogī who is not physically present, but appears somewhere in a mind-made form looking like his ordinary body, performs an act or delivers a message and then disappears again.

In one such experience I had in India, a yogī, of whose existence I had not before known, appeared to me in the middle of the night, told me who he was, gave me a message and then disappeared. Some time afterward, with the express intention of seeing him, I visited the remote village in which he lived, and found him there. This was not a case, as mentioned above, of a body becoming invisible.

III, 21. "Karma is (of two kinds), with commencement and without commencement; by Mind-poise on these, or from omens, there is knowledge of the latter end (i.e. death)."

The word karma has been used to such a great extent in English that it must by now be considered adopted into the language. I may here remind the reader that karmas are actions or works done or made by us in the past, the results of which are still to be faced in the future. All schools of Hindu thought are at one in the belief that after death (generally after some time) a man must return to earth to receive the results of all actions done with desire. His sufferings and misfortunes are considered to be due to his own faults—the reactions of injuries done to others through greed, pride, anger etc.—while his pleasures and good fortune are due to his past efforts in well-doing. There is thereby quite a store of karmas waiting their turn for most of us. I say most of us, because selfishness increases the store and unselfishness decreases it —the quantity of it is thereby a question of the weakening of the Sources of Trouble.

Sometime the series of lives will come to an end when, with the perfecting of character, which is synonymous with the complete destruction of the Sources of Trouble, there will be the cessation of the process of making karmas. This will be simultaneous with reaching the end of the store of karmas, inasmuch as the facing of karmas with full will, intelligence and love (by Body-conditioning, Self-study and Attentiveness to God) produces the character which is of the nature of freedom by uncovering the light. We shall come to the subject of freedom and release from the series of bodily lives later on, but in the meantime we must note that the proposed freedom is not a negative liberation or escape from bondage, nor a development or attainment of powers with which to overcome anything inimical outside or inside ourselves, but is rather of the nature of a discovery or self-revelation. Let the light shine. The light is self-sufficient.

The present aphorism tells us that the yogī can know the time of his death by Mind-poise upon two kinds of karma built into in his present bodily life—that is, what is in visible operation at the moment, and what is still in store to be dealt with in the current life-state and life-period, but has not yet come on. The idea is put in another way when it is said that of the group of karmas due to be faced in the present life-period and life-state some come on quickly and some slowly. This is volitional to the degree that by clearing away existing karmas with full will, love and thought, the yogī makes room for others to come on. On the other hand, it is considered that when the time of death is known in advance in accordance with the operation of karma, it is within the power of the yogī to change that time if he wishes to do so.

The belief is common in India that holy men often foretell their own deaths. We hear of cases of very peaceful deaths —the holy man takes leave of his disciples and friends, tells them that the time has come for him to go, and then quietly dies in his sleep or Meditation. The choice of karmas also occurs. I know of the case of an aspirant who was asked in Meditation when still quite a young boy to make the choice whether he would be tall or short in this life; he chose the latter and so it worked out. In another case the aspirant was informed in Meditation that a specific kind of illness was pending and asked whether he would take it in one burst or dribbled over a long time. He chose the long time, and so it occurred.

An indicator of the approaching end of life is here mentioned—omens or portents. It is not that the practice of the magical or occult arts is recommended for purposes of divination of the time of death, but that Mind-poise upon uncommon occurrences or omens leads to a knowledge of their meaning. "What does it mean," a lady asked me, "when I dream of a little white hen?" I was not able to tell her, but I believe that if I could have questioned her closely and found out whether it was in any way paranormal—an omen—we could have discovered its meaning in her mind-mixture and whether or not it was part of an integration-struggle using some psycho-hieroglyph. A Hindu "psychic" I met for the first time said, when I mentioned that I was going to depart from the town by a certain train, "Oh, no, you're not." I missed that train—an almost unprecedented occurrence for me. When afterward asked how he knew, this man said there were certain twitchings in his arm which meant yes or no, and they were always right. Such things were the basis of part of the old magic in many nations. A great amount of modern mediumship shows the same principle at work, a very intimate mixture of truth and error.

III, 22. "(From Mind-poise) on friendliness, etc. arise (various kinds of) strength."

In Patanjali's view—and I am profoundly sure that he was right—we can derive benefit, even ordinary strength, only from Contemplation of the good with a good heart. To look upon another's strength or prosperity with envy can give us no success; to contemplate it with gladness opens to us the mystery door to the same strength.

When the teacher here says "friendliness etc." his et cetera means compassion and gladness, as it has direct reference to another aphorism (I, 33)[1] in which he says that clearness or purity of mind results from regarding the happy with friendliness, the suffering with sympathy and the good with gladness, and not dwelling mentally upon the bad.

In our present aphorism, Patanjali speaks not merely of the cultivation of these virtues, but of Mind-poise upon them. The cultivation of them produces clearness of mind, but this practice of Mind-poise on them produces various kinds of strength, thus manifesting their power.

The progressing yogī is sometimes warned to be careful what he thinks or wishes, for it is found that even his comparatively casual desires awaken some inner power which definitely brings about material results. The yogī who is careful always to preserve these three emotions towards the happy, the suffering and the good, and to ignore the bad, may rapidly go forward from strength to strength without any fear of harm.

In the next aphorism Patanjali again reminds us of the importance of attention to the concrete. There is little use in

[1] See Chapter 17.

thinking of strength, goodness, truth, beauty and other abstractions without basing the thought upon examples actually experienced. To poise upon strength, for example, he tells the learner to think of an elephant.

III, 23. "(From Mind-poise) upon (various kinds of) strengths arise the strength of an elephant, etc."

There are accounts of yogīs who, when they wanted, could stand or sit so firmly that a dozen strong men could not move them at all, also of cases in which they could move or bear very great weights. The et cetera in this aphorism is taken to mean that the yogī can similarly acquire the different powers exemplified by all kinds of animals.

Next comes a statement about general clairvoyance:

III, 24. "By putting forth advanced sight comes knowledge of the minutely small, the concealed and the distant."

As an example of such clairvoyance, I may mention that once when I went with an old Indian friend to visit a certain yogī about eighty miles from Madras, we traveled to several villages to find him, and at the end, when we did so, he at once told us he had seen us coming and gave us an account of our travels.

It is generally difficult to distinguish clairvoyance from thought-transference. As an example of this process, I will give an experience of one of my uncles when I was a boy. He occasionally visited a clairvoyant in Manchester, England, whom he knew quite well. Once the clairvoyant told him that he could see a convict looking through some bars and seemingly wanting to say something, and flew to the conclusion that this was a vision of a departed relative. My uncle had been to a wax-work show where such a figure was on exhibition; he had in the meantime quite forgotten the incident, but the clairvoyant somehow caught it up from the recesses of his mind.

As an instance of seeing the concealed, I recall some experiments in which I took part about forty years ago, wherein a clairvoyant read some words written inside sealed envelopes.

There is quite a big modern literature on this subject. In particular I would mention the numerous accounts in M. Camille Flammarion's *After Death*, in which there are descriptions of domestic animals as well as human beings seeing apparitions, mostly of the recently dead. My own paternal grandmother suddenly exclaimed in the presence of several members of our family: "Oh, Chris is drowning!" She said that she saw him (her brother) struggling in the water. News came later that he had been drowned near Liverpool just at that time.

Patanjali now gives a number of examples of the effects of poise, which I may group together. They are intended, I think, merely as examples, as at the end of them he says that any other objects may be used.

III, 25. *"From Mind-poise on the sun comes knowledge of the inhabited regions."*

III, 26. *"On the moon, knowledge of the array of stars."*

III, 27. *"On the pole-star, knowledge of their motions."*

III, 28. *"On the center at the navel, knowledge of the arrangement of the body."*

III, 29. *"On the pit of the throat, the cessation of hunger and thirst."*

III, 30. *"On the 'tortoise-tube,' steadiness."*

III, 31. *"On the light in the head, seeing of the adepts."*

III, 32. *"Or, from intuition, (knowledge) of all things."*

In III, 25 to III, 30 above, we have examples of starting points for psychometric knowledge. The tortoise-tube is held to be a cavity in the chest, below the pit of the throat, having the shape of a tortoise. Perhaps it refers to the lungs.

III, 33. "In the heart, understanding of the mind."

I have separated III, 33 from the previous group as I do not want to translate it as "on the heart," but "in the heart." Meditation on the heart may interfere with its function. Although it is possible thus to control the heart and even stop its beating for a little while—I have seen this done—that is not the object of yoga. But instead of, as normally, feeling oneself as centered somewhere between and behind the eyebrows, one can transfer oneself to the heart, and there watch the play of ideas in the mind. It is to be noted that the Mind-poises mentioned are generally upon objects or upon ideas in the mind, but in this case it is not knowledge that is to be attained, but understanding. In practice, meditation in the heart gives knowledge of the feelings of oneself and others, which the habit of head-meditation, with its mental linkages with eyesight, is apt to overlook. The introduction of feeling into knowledge, that is sensitiveness to life, not merely to objective fact, gives a deeper understanding of things and persons.

There is a school of yoga, closely associated with the Hatha Yoga, which prescribes a series of meditations in what are called the centers (*chakras*). Six of these centers are mentioned, strung upon a triple cord which passes up the spine from the base of it to the brain. These centers are at about the level of (1) the anus, (2) the genitals, (3) the navel, (4) the heart, (5) the throat, and (6) the eyes. A great force called "the coiled" (*kundalini*) is described as residing in the first center (but sometimes in the third), and as being roused by certain kinds of meditation, whereupon it uncoils and rushes up a channel within the cord and out at the top of the head, and the man then falls into a trance. The object is, however, to meditate in such a manner that this coiled force is under the control of the will and is led into each center in turn, so that its owner can develop the psychic powers associated with each of them. The centers are described as normally appearing like flowers, each having a certain number of petals, with downward-turned faces, which turn upward when the coiled force comes to reside in them for the period of meditation in the center. The culmination of the whole process arrives when the coiled force is taken beyond all the six centers into the "thousand-petaled lotus" in the top part of the head, where it confers upon the man the highest intuitions and realizations. The name Laya Yoga (*laya* means latent) is given to this method, as it uses the coiled force latent in the body.

Patanjali does not refer to this force or method, and when, as in III, 28 and III, 29, and III, 33, above, he speaks of Mind-poise at navel, throat and heart, there is no reason to assume that he is making reference to the centers dealt with in the Laya Yoga system. Here, as always, Patanjali follows the Rāja Yoga method of laying all the stress upon control from within, and not recommending any processes for influencing or "helping" the mind from the body. In Rāja Yoga it is axiomatic that body should follow mind, not the reverse.

Supplementary note to Chapter 12.

It is often useful, even in ordinary actions, to "put the consciousness" in the working part. For example, when walking along the road, to be "conscious in the hips" gives a new poise and ease of motion, and overcomes shuffling or falling along and "shoulder-walking." When practicing regular breathing, we may similarly, put our consciousness in our lung-mechanism. We can move ourselves from place to place within both body and mind.

CHAPTER 13

GREATER POWERS

Before giving another series of still more advanced psychic powers mentioned by Patanjali as attainable by Concentration, Meditation and Contemplation, I will quote an isolated statement which appears as his first aphorism in Book IV.

IV, 1. "The psychic powers are produced at birth, and by drugs, incantations, asceticism and Contemplation."

In many people quite marked psychic powers are natural, derived from heredity or, as the Hindus generally believe, because they are brought over from previous lives in which they have been cultivated. Most people have at least some small paranormal experience in their lives, and some races, such as the Celtic peoples, are generally credited with more than the average of this tendency.

Among the other four cases mentioned—by drugs, incantations, asceticism and Contemplation—Patanjali gives directions only for the use of Contemplation. We are led to feel that he did not approve of drugs, incantations, or asceticism for this purpose. We must note, I think, that only a great use of drugs, incantations and asceticism would produce any decisive effects. The ordinary use of drugs gives rise to abnormal dreams; but there are also drugs which induce mediumship, trance and clairvoyance such as those sometimes produced by hypnotism. The ordinary use of repetitive songs, such as hymns, can produce exaltation, but the systematic and intensive use of sounds in incantation goes far beyond that and does produce results. Indeed, I have seen a yogī produce a shower of rain over a large field with the aid of drum-beating and very intensive and prolonged incantations. The ordinary use of all the means for ensuring the welfare and purification of the body, already described as Body-conditioning, one of the three observances enjoined on the would-be yogī in the beginning, is very far from that excess of the same which is called austerity, which by attenuating the physical body does lay it open readily to psychic impressions. I have allowed myself to translate the word as austerity in this case, because excessive severity on the body is enjoined among those who wish to use Body-conditioning as their chief means of obtaining psychic powers.

Patanjali does not say that all these means can produce all the powers. The general belief among yogīs and the Hindu public is that drugs, incantations and asceticism can produce only some of them, and those not lofty nor admirable, and that only Contemplation can bring about really notable powers.

I now give another group of powers, which on the whole are more intimate to the yogī's growth or progress than those given in the last chapter.

III, 37. "The mind can enter another's body when there is a loosening of the causes of bondage and also knowledge of the procedure."

Loosening of the causes of bondage refers to the weakening of Sources of Trouble and the karmas, these being the two things which cause attachment, as we have seen in an earlier chapter. Knowledge of the procedure is considered to arise as an intuition resulting from Contemplation. The meaning of the aphorism is that, given these two conditions, the yogī can leave his own body or go into a "brown study" and enter the body of another person with or without dispossession of the original owner. For example, a lecturer could be assisted in this way by a yogī knowing how to do it.

I remember well a statement, which I was not in a position

to verify, about an expert in yoga who was getting old and thinking of letting go of the body. It happened just then that a boy was drowned somewhere in the Punjab. The expert saw this by clairvoyance, saw also that the boy's body was suitable. Two things then happened—the expert died very suddenly and the boy was resuscitated and showed new and striking traits of character, which later led him to give up the normal course of life and join some yogīs living further north.

It is generally believed also that persons who are very intent upon some work of philanthropy, or science or art, and who die feeling keenly that their work is unfinished, can sometimes miss what is regarded as the usual course of subjective after-death existence and return at once to a suitable birth without any change of mind-contents.

III, 38. "From control of the 'upward air' comes freedom from contact with water, mud, thorns, and similar things, and the power to rise up."

What is referred to here as the upward air is one of what are called the five "vital airs." Advanced yogīs are credited with the ability to recognize these "vital airs" in the body, and to be able to control them. In the Hatha Yoga schools—distinguished from the Rāja Yoga schools of Patanjali and others, as I have before observed, by their working on the body to affect the mind, instead of in the reverse way—much is made of these "vital airs." In one of the principal Hatha Yoga works, four of them are described as active in the regions of the heart, the anus, the navel and the throat, while the fifth moves all over the body. Some say that the first operates from the nose down to the heart—vitalizing; the second, which is concerned with excretion, works from as high as the navel to as low as the soles of the feet; the third, which has to do with digestion of food, acts from the heart to the navel; the fourth, which carries upward and is concerned with speech, manifests from the heart to the head; and the fifth operates all over the body as distributor of energy.

The idea of the present aphorism is that the yogī who has learned to control the "upward air" can walk on water without being wet; on mud without being soiled; on thorns and such things without being hurt; and can, if he wishes, float across ravines without needing a bridge.

III, 39. "From control of the 'equalizing air' comes brightness."

This vital air, being concerned with digestion, is considered to be connected with heat and fire. In the present event, it is held that digestion will be perfect and the whole body will have a shining quality.

III, 40. "From Mind-poise upon the connection between the ear and the ether arises higher hearing."

What I have here translated ether is not thought of as empty space, but as a continuous reality or substance which lies between things, and keeps them apart, but offers no obstruction to any movement. The idea of empty space never appealed to Hindu minds. They long ago classed substances or states of matter as five, namely: earth, water, fire, air and ether. These all have the nature of substance, that is, each of them has a class-connotation, and is marked by certain qualities and activities. They are regarded as associated respectively with the senses of smell, taste, sight, touch and hearing. The last runs counter to our modern knowledge that sound is not conveyed in the absence of solids, liquids and gases. It may be mentioned that paranormal sensations, including clairaudience, are all conveyed without the aid of their normal substances. Clairvoyance thus operates without light (fire).

III, 41. "From Mind-poise upon the connection between the body and the ether and from (Mind-poise upon) the attainment of the lightness of cotton, arises traveling in the ether."

It may be asked whether Patanjali means that the body can pass through the ether, or that a mind-body is formed for this purpose; the form of the following aphorism indicates the latter.

III, 42. "In external, not fanciful, form it is 'the great disembodiment'; from that there is diminution of the covering of the light."

In modern English this is called traveling in the astral body, astral meaning nothing more than starry in the sense of carrying its own light. In an earlier chapter I have recorded one experience of my own in which a practicing yogī visited me in such a form, from a distance of over two hundred miles. I have other similar experiences in mind, in which other varieties of this psychic power may have been used. Let me try to classify the principal varieties: (*a*) The yogī forms his mind-body and goes out in it, leaving his body asleep or in trance, or a very "brown study." (*b*) He forms a mind-body for a limited purpose, ensouls it with a thought-form and sends it off to do its work, including perhaps appearing to someone in this form. (*c*) He establishes a permanent thought-transferring link with a mind-body of himself produced and preserved mainly by the thoughts of someone with whom he wants to keep in communication. This occurs often between yoga-teacher and pupil, and is not strictly a form of traveling in the ether.

All these are held to involve a diminution of the covering of the light. Inasmuch as there is less obscuration of sense faculties and an absence of darkness in this condition, there is less covering of the light. But if we are thinking of the true light of the real man, we must remember that this psychic power, like all the others, contains the dangers of attachment to pleasures and personal pride, which may be serious obstacles in the way of attaining that, which is final independence (*kaivalya*). All this depends upon the feelings and motives with which the powers are used directly or indirectly to affect persons and things.

III, 43. "Control of the forms of matter (i.e. elements) arises from Mind-poise on their solid state, character, finer forms, connections and utility or function."

There are five forms of matter and each has five aspects, through which the yogī will work his way if he wishes to meditate upon them. Each of the five can be considered first in its ordinary obvious form—for example, a piece of earth in its ordinary solid appearance. As regards character, it has smell, constancy in the form of atoms and inconstancy in compounds and various other forms including the body and the sense organs. Next, we think of the finer structure so well known to us these days from the researches of our physicists, or its ancient Hindu equivalent, the subtle and normally unseen constituents. Fourthly, its connections and relations to the others, beginning with its relation to the fundamental qualities of nature—matter, energy and law. Fifthly, what purpose it serves, including the part it plays in the education and final emancipation of men. Such is a skeletal sketch of the course of a Meditation, the results of which are control of matter and the ability to make and unmake forms. Under this head come dematerialization and rematerialization.

A very trustworthy friend of mine told me of an experience of his own in this connection. A yogī paid a visit to his bungalow, and in the course of discussion said he would show him and the few friends who were there some phenomena of this kind. First, he took them to a vegetable market not far away and they selected a variety of vegetables, paid for them, and put them aside, telling the storekeeper that they would get them afterward. The friends then returned to the bungalow and sat on a terrace in front of the door. Then the yogī said, "Which will you have first?" and when my friend replied, "Oh, some potatoes," the yogī meditated a moment and then made a sign with his hand, and there were the potatoes lying on the terrace. In this way, all the purchased vegetables were brought home, and afterward they were kept, cooked and eaten.

Practical Americans will at once ask, "Why did not these yogīs long ago give us all the information in chemistry and physics that we have toiled so long to obtain, and why did they not do something to make their country prosperous?" The answer is simple: Their minds did not turn that way. They are not interested in prosperity, but in liberation from the wheel of births and deaths, and they hold that the real fruit of human experience and development can be more easily obtained in a Hindu village than in all the multifariousness of Western life. "The simple things are best," they say. They have not the least desire for modern plumbing and motor cars, and in the rare cases in which they can be induced to give an opinion about modern life, if they have come to know anything about it, they are inclined to say that the "Europeans" are apt to mistake comfort for progress, and even then, while they get comfort in some ways they lose it in others. It is all the difference between the introvert and the extrovert.

Patanjali continues with a statement of further attainments which arise from the yogī's pursuit of Meditation on the same line:

III, 44. "*From that come into existence minuteness etc. and excellence of the body, and absence of resistance from their (i.e. the elements') qualities.*"

III, 45. "*Excellence of the body consists of correct form, beauty, strength and very firm well-knitness.*"

These things can be brought about by the yogī because of his control of the elements described in III, 43. Earth, water, fire, air and ether and their qualities will not obstruct him in these great undertakings.

Minuteness etc. refers to a standard set of eight psychic powers, which are:

(1) smallness (*animā*): to become very small at will;
(2) bigness (*mahimā*): to become very big at will;
(3) lightness (*laghimā*): to become very light at will;
(4) heaviness (*garimā*): to become very heavy at will;
(5) reach (*prāpti*): to be able to obtain anything;
(6) free will (*prākāmya*): whereby there is no restraint;
(7) creativeness (*īshatwa*): the power to make things; and
(8) mastery (*vashitwa*): the power to direct them.

Having finished with the substances or elements, Patanjali now turns to the senses and deals with them in the same manner:

III, 46. *"Control of the senses comes from Mind-poise on their function, character, individuality, connections and utility."*

III, 47. *"From that comes quickness as of the mind, sensing without organs and control of substances."*

Just as in III, 43 five aspects of each of the elements were considered, so here we have five aspects of each of the senses. First there is sense-ness; then the character of each, which we find in sounds, sights, odors, etc.; then their individual nature —the sensation of sound, for example, being totally different from the sensation of color, these "personalities" being their subtle character, so to speak; then, fourthly, their connections; and finally, the part they play in knowledge and in the education of man.

CHAPTER 14

PREPARING FOR FREEDOM

There is a familiar Hindu proverb which asserts: "Ripe fruit will not remain upon the branch," and another which alludes to the fact that in ripe fruit the stone or seed ceases to stick to the pulp, and becomes detached from it quite easily. These proverbs are specifically applied to the human state, and refer to the idea that sooner or later every man will become satiated not only with the ordinary pleasures of life but even with those greater ones which the psychic powers can bring. This satiation is not a bad thing. It is an indication that the man is becoming "ripe," ready to drop from the branch of the tree of human incarnations. He is, in terms of Patanjali's philosophy, near to Independence (*kaivalya*), which some other schools call freedom (*moksha*), and the Buddhists name *nirvāna*.

The same proverb is frequently used to admonish the aspirant who is impatient to reach the end of his work, or is despondent at the thought of the long time that he thinks it will take him to do so. It accompanies the advice to stop thinking about success, the future, and time, and simply to do the work and live the life of the present. It is folly to waste this precious present moment, and the ripening can be trusted to take care of itself and occur without fail when it ought to do so.

Following upon the psychic powers mentioned in the last two chapters, Patanjali treats of the outlook of the man who has reached or nearly reached this ripeness:

III, 48. "In the case of him who has reached as far as the knowledge of the otherness of the pure mind and the real man, there is mastery in all states of existence, and knowership with regard to all."

Even the conception of the pure mind must not be attributed to the real man. When the yogī realizes this he has come to the last thing that can be mistaken for the real self, so nothing that exists can now hold and bind him. This is called the sorrowless condition.

III, 49. "When the seeds of bondage have been destroyed by his being uncolored even by that (i.e. the pure mind), there will be Independence."

The seeds are the Sources of Trouble and the karmas, but when there is no response in the yogī to the attractions and repulsions of the world, because he has no longer any desire for them and is not colored by them, the seeds are spoken of as being scorched in the fire of knowledge, so that now they cannot germinate and grow. This uncoloredness cannot be intellectual merely, and it cannot be forced, but must depend upon the ripeness of experience. Even the greatest temptation must fail to stir the yogī. The teacher thinks of the greatest external lure he can, and says:

III, 50. "If there is an invitation from the deities presiding over some place, it must be no cause for proud concurrence, for there may (thus) be renewed contact with what is not wanted."

Patanjali is still thinking of the yogī as understanding the conditions required for Independence, mentioned in the previous aphorism, and as being very near the goal but not yet there, so he now brings up the important subject of Discrimination between even the highest objective experience and condition and the state of the real man.

III, 51. "From Mind-poise on moments and their succession arises the knowledge produced by Discrimination."

III, 52. "From this comes perception (as to which is which) of two equals which are not marked off as different by their classes, specific characters or positions."

In ordinary knowledge two things are known by comparison of their different classes, as "This is a cow and that is a pot"; or, if they are of the same class, by their specific differences, as "This is a red cow and that is a white cow"; or, if they have the same specific character, by their position in space or time, as "This is the red cow in the field, and that is the red cow on the road." But suppose these two cows are moved about when the observer is not looking, he will not be able to recognize which was which when he looks at them again, they perhaps not being in the same places this moment as they were in the earlier moment.

Now, a moment is a portion of time in which there is no time. It is conceived of as the actual present, which occupies no time but only a moment. In such a moment there can be no change, for if there were a change it would be two moments, not one. So it is the unit of time, in which time stands still, and what we commonly call time is really an idea of a succession of moments.

Next, the only way to reach a perception of two things which have the same class appearance, specific character appearance, and position appearance, though they are not really the same, as in the present case of the pure mind and the man, is by an intuitive knowledge to be obtained by Mind-poise. Such is the nature of Discrimination, which is not ratiocination but intuition. As the real man is not an object of knowledge, but the pure mind is, and the former is not subject to moments and successions but the latter is, Mind-poise on this point must be resorted to for realization of the difference.

III, 53. "And, the intuitional, which is knowledge produced by Discrimination, has all things for its objects, and all times for its objects, but is without succession."

The attainment of intuition of any kind or degree depends upon the purity of motive of the observer. In this case, perfect Discrimination depends upon the pure mind, and:

III, 54. "When there is equality of purity of the pure mind and the real man, there is Independence."

This comes at the end of Patanjali's Book III. He devotes all the fourth and last book to the same subject in greater detail, covering, indeed, the whole ground of the relations between man, mind and the world. I will make this the subject of my next chapters.

CHAPTER 15

THE HUMAN LIFE CYCLE

Patanjali assumes a certain cultural background and ideology in his pupils. He assumes as part of this the belief that the mind of man goes through a series of incarnations in bodies, in the course of which that mind gains more and more mastery over itself and the world. He assumes that this cycle of incarnations is not prescribed by a deity, who has built the world as a kind of school for us and arranged a series of classes and grades, through which we must go, but that these incarnations are the result of our own impulses.

Though the mind, he believes, has no external limits, it limits itself at any given time to certain interests. In short, it desires certain experiences, and becomes so involved in them emotionally and mentally that only a course of yoga can extract it. It works for certain things and gets what it works for, either by making them itself or getting them from other people. In getting things from others it sometimes inflicts pain, and then it gets that pain in some way, for it has made pain. If it has made pleasurable things for others, it will also experience pleasure. The things it works for and gets and the experiences of pain and pleasure coming from its transactions with other people are called its karmas. As long as it deals with these karmas from the standpoint of their pleasurableness or painfulness it will go on making new karmas. But suppose by yoga it stops this cycle of karmas and of births and deaths, and resumes its unlimited form; that will lead to rapid liberation, or Independence. All this I have mentioned before, but now we must study it a little closer.

Now I will turn the light of modern as well as ancient psychological knowledge on this process. We ask ourselves what it is that causes the mind to want these limited experiences, and we turn to experience itself for our answer. A little boy hears a sound of bells moving along the street. He knows that sound is made by the ice-cream man. He thinks of ice cream and the pleasure of eating it. Is he satisfied with that mental picture? No; he reaches for a ten-cent piece, runs out into the street, gets his ice cream and starts nibbling little pieces off it. What pleasure! Why? The answer is: Because he feels an enhancement of life. He is at the moment being more alive than before; in this experience there is life-expansion, though he does not think of this and is not aware of it.

In our schooldays fifty years ago we were taught that self-preservation is the first law of Nature and is, in fact, the mark or sign of life. Soon we learned that self-preservation does not satisfy the living creature; it wants self-expansion, more life. More life does not at once come with more expanded experience, but with intensified experience, narrowed, one-pointed, concentrated or attentive experience. Embodied life gives us this. Disembodiedment of mind—if we imagine such a thing for a moment—would leave us vague, indefinite, unsatisfied. We seek these narrow, intense experiences because they wake up our life and give us the pleasant feeling of self-expansion.

The feeling of unimpeded expanding life is pleasure. In the body it goes with health, which is the non-obstruction of balanced functions and enhanced activity and relaxation. In the mind, it is found in clearness—an absence of clutter and confusion—and in the process of thinking, which begins with concentration. Self-expansion does not mean the *thought,* "I am more," but the feeling of life enhanced or increased in some way. Also it does not mean material increase, in body or mind. Concentration or focusing is expansion of life. Enhancement might be a better term to use, but the word expansion is well established. As we need material objects to help in the focusing and concentrating of mind (the turning of the whole of itself upon a part of itself) we seek objects which are limiting, and in some cases even painful—but not too painful —for this gain.

It is as the idea of self grows, and with it the pride of self-personality, that we get artificial or mental contraction and expansion. Men make idols of themselves in thought. More money, power over others, fame, name, work, knowledge, even vice and virtue, in brief, greatness or great-littleness— in these things life is now felt, and the ice cream and common-sense appreciation of bodily health and pleasure drop out of focus, like the taste of the cup of coffee that I forgot to notice. There comes up also a further refinement—a dream within a dream, so to speak—when people attach themselves mentally to the greatness of others, and suffer greatly if their idea of these becomes smirched by fact, deflated or debunked. But I must not now go too far into the examination of these refinements, as this is not intended to be an essay on the psychopathic condition of normal civilized life. For understanding the essential principle of life-expansion or self-expansion or enhancement, let us return to the illustration of the little boy and his ice cream.

This experience does not merely arrive, give pleasure or pain, and then pass away. It leaves its mark upon the mind. It leaves conscious and subconscious impulses connected with its mark on the mind, for in such seeking and in the endeavor to get the most out of an experience the mind has used and developed its powers. This goes far beyond the mere enjoyment of ice cream. The time comes when the mind will pursue creative impulses, the desires of the artist, the social organizer, the scientist and many others. The powers of the mind grow, so that now it can grasp larger and more complicated things and ideas with a clearness and intensity that earlier it could get only with little things. The mind can turn its attention to its own powers and its own growth and make great strides in these by self-cultivation.

It is here that I may say that it does not matter much in practice whether we regard Patanjali and his pupils as right or wrong in their belief in a succession of bodily lives, for the benefit of every yoga practice is obtained from the doing of it. We are concerned in the enrichment of our lives—that means, of our powers—as long as we are alive and can attend to that. Only, Patanjali presents a goal and says, in effect, "If you don't reach this goal in the present body you will have future opportunities in future bodies until you do reach it. That goal is a state of consciousness fully clear and strong, without the necessity of limitation or concentration." He cannot credit this to a mind whose very business is a process of repeated contraction and expansion. So, in the end it is the man who stands forth in his full power and light of unobstructed consciousness, without the need of world, or body, or mind.

In the course of yoga, Patanjali gives a bit of practice and then a bit of theory, then more practice and so on, in the best tradition of teaching. At the point we have reached in the aphorisms, the pupil has strengthened his mind very greatly. Contemplation and Mind-poise are now easy for him; he is almost at that point of self-culture at which he will exchange mind-life for man-life, or pass from man-man to god-man. But he knows that he still needs some experience—some karmas are still to be dealt with, and they would not be there but for his need of the experience they can give, so he is ready to face them, and now Patanjali brings in the idea—startling to many people—that the yogī can face them quickly by living in several bodies all at the same time. We will resume our study of the aphorisms:

IV, 2. *"Transformation into another condition of life is by the inflow of Nature."*

Transformation into another condition of life means coming into a new body. This has been described in connection with II, 12 and II, 13, as resulting from good and bad actions or karmas. It is generally held that a person cannot live more than one life at a time, except in the case of yogīs, who are able to do so through a certain form of Contemplation. In either case the cause of the particular embodiment is the karmas. Patanjali reminds us here that Nature is the material cause or basis of all forms. He explains in the next aphorism the part played by the karmas, called the instrumental or efficient cause:

IV, 3. "*The instrumental cause is not the director of Nature, but from it comes the removal of obstacles, as in the case of the cultivator of a field.*"

In India it is common to see men at work cultivating the fields, and often supplying water to channels which have been prepared beforehand. At one point a man will be in charge of one or two bulls which are harnessed to a rope passing over a wheel and down into a large well, where it ends in a big vessel made partly of iron and partly of leather. From the side of the well there is a long slope, down which the bulls walk as they draw up the water. When the water arrives it pours out—perhaps as much as forty gallons at a time—into the prepared channels. Another man is moving about in the field, letting the water first into one branch and then into another, by means of handfuls of clay which he puts in or removes, as required. This is the allusion in the aphorism. The good and bad deeds do not produce the new conditions of life—those are just a part of Nature's flow—but they act as the instrumental cause by removing the obstruction so that the flow will go in a certain way.

We know very well in modern Western life that in most of our human operations we do very little ourselves, but by small arrangements we give a turn to great forces of Nature and produce prodigious effects. I like to contemplate the powers of the mind as being of this kind also. The actual energy of concentrated thought must be very small indeed, but its touch on the fine and hidden levers in the body has everything to do with all the success in our lives, and it can operate in some measure externally from the body as well, as is well proved in thought transference and other powers. But now, back to our yogī and his working out of his life.

IV, 4. *"The artificial minds arise only from the self-personality."*

IV, 5. *"One mind is the director of the several, in their divided business."*

Whatever Self-personality may remain with the yogī is the measure of the minds which he provides for his extra bodies. He does not make minds with a different kind of personality from his own—that is the meaning.

I have no personal experience of these duplications, but I have heard they are supposed to be very limited in their interests and versatility. They are regarded as really outposts of the yogī's own mind and, though carrying on rather mechanically, are available to his full presence or influence whenever he chooses. The karmas met and dealt with in these bodies must have their effect on the yogī himself, if he is to deal with them, get his good from them, and eventually discharge them.

IV, 6. *"In this case (a mind) produced by Meditation is without a receptacle (for karmas)."*

That is, it does not accumulate karmas for future treatment. When it deals with any experience it passes the results on to the mind of the yogī himself. The yogī is meeting his lessons of karma without personal desires, and so without adding to his karmas for the future. His actions are described as neither white nor black, that is, not producing either good or bad consequences to himself. The theory of renunciation among the Hindus is that actions done or life lived without any personal motive produce no karmic results.

IV, 7. *"The karma of a yogī is neither white nor black. Of others it is of three kinds."*

IV, 8. *"From those, there is the manifestation only of those latencies which are suitable for ripening."*

The three kinds are good (producing pleasant karmic results), bad (leading to painful karmas), and mixed (having something of each). In any particular incarnation, with its kind of body and status, only a selection of the karmas will fit in together and thus be suitable for ripening. It is with the object of clearing up some more of those impending karmas that the advanced yogīs are said sometimes to provide themselves with extra bodies and subsidiary minds.

IV, 9. *"Even when they (i.e. the latencies) are obstructed by life-condition, place and time, they are still within, because habit-molds are similar to memories."*

IV, 10. *"And they are beginningless, as the wish to live is eternal."*

Habit in the body and memory in the mind, even though deep in the subconscious, as we now name it, are not lost; the old impressions are there and will come to the surface when circumstances are favorable. Therefore, it is held, results of actions, or karmas, are never lost, though they may be in suspension for a while. In connection with the practical study of hypnotism, it has been asserted that the whole of a person's experience is retained in the depth of memory and can be recovered by awakening suitable trains of thought.

The idea behind the word eternal as used by Patanjali must be studied for a moment. It does not mean something that will go on through all the future and has gone on all through the past. It means that without desire of life—desire for ice cream or something else—there simply would be no world with objects having limitations or characteristics of space and time. Desire does not begin at some point of time. It makes time-things and concentrates itself in them.

IV, 11. "Because it (the latent) is held together by cause, effect, receptacle and object, it is absent when these are absent."

The question arises: In what do the latencies inhere? The answer is: In the eternal desire to live. The next question is: In what does the eternal desire to live inhere? The answer is: The word "what" vitiates the question, for any "what" is not eternal. What we must say is that in some unthinkable way it belongs to the real man.

Now I add my own understanding of this matter, and say: This eternal desire to live, when subject to Ignorance and other Sources of Trouble and the ideas and karmas which they produce, manifests as life, actual and latent. Some part is latent because proper attention can be given only to a small part at once. The active are karmas. The latent exists within, as fulfilling a cause, having to produce an effect, being subject to storage, and depending on an object. These are here called briefly cause, effect, receptacle and object—cause being good or bad action; effect being pleasant or painful experience; receptacle being the subconscious mind side of the created expression or body; and object the external object which has to be met as experience. Put in simple words: there is karma when the present fruit of a past action appears in the meeting of a personality and its experience. Latency is waiting the opportunity for this manifestation, as in the case of memory, in which something is forgotten but can be recalled later on.

When, however, the yogī, through the destruction of Ignorance and the other Sources of Trouble, makes his actions seedless or without fruit, there comes about the absence of the four causes, and so the absence of the latencies.

*IV, 12. "What has gone and what is to come exist in their own
forms, because of the differences of the paths (or modes)
of their characters."*

Our words "past" and "future" would be inexact transla-
tions here, being too abstract. The aphorism definitely speaks
of "the gone" and "the not-come." It is here said that when we
think of what has gone and what is to come we are thinking
of something real. That does not mean that they have the
same kind of reality as what is present, or that we must try to
think of them as existing in the same way or mode as that. I
may repeat here that the present is as much unknown as the
past or the future, both to our senses and to our thought, and
in practice every one of our perceptions or observations involves a mental grasp of more than the present. Let us credit
all the three with reality, but each with its own kind of character.

In practice, the past is a causal push and the future a causal
pull. When I contemplate a tiny seed sprouting and growing
into a tree of a particular kind, I cannot imagine its very be-
ginnings, seed within seed, and seed within seed, ad infini-
tum, as being a kind of coiled spring in the uncoiling of which
the tree must arise, nor on the other hand that it is the pull
of the perfect tree that is the sole cause of the growth; nevertheless the latter view has some preferential claims to greater
probability, inasmuch as nothing comes out of nothing and
potentiality of any kind is something real.

If you say that what is present can hit us on the nose and
make it bleed, while what is in the past and in the future cannot do so, I reply: "Yes, that is one form of reality, but do not
deny the other forms as well, which have their say in the
process of causality which produces all the fleeting presents,
including that which just now bumped me on the nose and
then went its way."

If the real man wanted to see the effect in mind of the

bump on the nose of its body he could do so, could he not? And if he has the purpose of producing some change (which yet we must not call change) in himself through a karmic cycle of experience, who is to say him nay and deny to him some will power (which yet we must not call either will or power) which is nothing but the creative influence of the future upon the present?

IV, 13. *"They are manifest and subtle, and have the nature of the Qualities."*

Manifest refers to what is grasped by our senses, what we think of as in the present. This includes touch as well as sight, etc. Touch needs special mention, because it is more closely associated with reality in our common thinking than any other of the senses. It is in connection with touch (as in the bump on the nose) that we experience the materiality of matter, that is, the irrefutable resistivity of material forms of the grade of our bodies. Subtle means those realities which are outside the range of our senses, but are knowable to the mind. Ordinarily their reality is known to the mind by their causality, but in contemplation their presence is said to be knowable directly. What the present aphorism states is that all of them (gone, existing and to come) have the nature of the three Qualities. They are all thought of as real in a real objective world and as composed in various ways of the three strands of the cloth of Nature—matter, energy and law.

Supplementary note to Chapter 15.

The awareness of a mind by other minds was also referred to in III, 19 (page 163). Sympathy, affection, goodwill: all contain this "telepathy." The process begins in a mental noticing of the expression on the features of another, and then, when good feeling is allowed to arise, this opens up the telepathic avenues of love-knowledge. This is the direct knowledge of minds by minds, and is the essence of love.

CHAPTER 16

MAN, MIND AND WORLD

I will here remind the reader of Patanjali's statement (I, 4) that when the ideas in the mind are controlled the man stands in his own true state of being, but otherwise he is surrendered to circumstances. These circumstances are not merely the facts of life and the world, but also and even more the ideas in the mind.

My object is to point out that the practice of yoga and the attainment of its end or goal do not change the real man. At least the declaration is that the man is the unchanging witness or observer of all these occurrences. His nature is such as to be beyond anything we can think of as change. We must not anthropomorphize ourselves, or imagine our real selves to be what we seem to ourselves to be.

Really, we are here face to face with the principle, which I have mentioned before, that when seeking intuition on any subject or uncovering the light in yoga we must never predict the results. We cannot say and must not think that when Independence is attained a change will take place in the real man. Something, yes, but we must not taint it by any comparison with the phenomena we meet in ordinary life or even in the process of yoga—not even the idea of change.

An attempt to certify—I cannot say define—this situation of the real man is sometimes made by the assertion that the witness or knower cannot change, for he would thereby become a thing known, and thus cease to be the knower. The real man will never be the known. We cannot "see him," but we can let him realize himself.

I can perhaps elucidate the principle a little more by reference to Buddhist teaching. The followers of that religion are advised not even to think of the real man, for even that idea carries the taint of earth, so to speak. There must be no anthropomorphism at all in the idea of what the Buddhists call *nirvāna*. In their conception, the man who pursues the ordinary course of the series of lives in bodily form is only a bundle of habit-molds. He is undergoing gradual change—something is constantly being chipped off, something else constantly added to him, as his Sources of Trouble attach him to karmas, and this wheel of life goes on revolving until (by first weakening and then destroying the Sources of Trouble) he reaches *nirvāna*—but no one must attempt to define *nirvāna*. To think of it is to shut ourselves out of it or—a more appropriate simile—to go into a cave with a lighted candle to seek the sun. This simile is appropriate because the word *nirvāna* means a blowing out. We have to blow out the candlelight of false knowledge. In all this we see how careful Buddha was, so much so that he told us not to believe in the permanence of man. "Not him, nor any light shall gazer see with mortal eyes."

As I have here been led into reference to another school of thought than that of Patanjali, I must add that Hindus generally are able to use the imagination as a ladder and then kick it away. Patanjali does this with his real man, as I will presently show. In the Advaita Vedanta school of Shankarāchārya the same principle holds. The teacher there permits the pupil to think of what is called the manifested Brahman, provided he remembers that he will cast that erroneous idea aside when he is strong enough. Some of the later Buddhist thinkers also permitted the introduction of a "god-who-is-seen" (*avalokiteshwara*), who must however be transcended for the attainment of *nirvāna*.

These remarks of mine will introduce a series of aphorisms

(IV, 14-34) in which Patanjali expounds his theory of man, mind and world.

IV, 14. *"Things are real, because of unity within the transformations."*

Patanjali here subscribes to the same theory as we have in modern physics. An object undergoes a change in form, that is a transformation, but there is a continuity of substance, as, for example, when a lump of clay is molded and baked into a pot. That substance is real. When there is actually a removal of some substance from a thing—for example, if in the summer the sleeves are cut out of a dress—we still say it is the same dress, which is not perfectly accurate for science (as the substratum is not fully the same) but is true for ordinary purposes. There is the famous example of the old buggy, which had its wheels replaced by new ones at one time, its shafts at another, its sides at another, and, in fact, was so changed in course of time that not one bit of the original remained, and yet it continued to be referred to as the same old buggy. Here, too, there is a continuity of reality, because the parts are real substance, though suffering a change of place and attachment. Modern physics does not yet know what that substance is fundamentally, though every now and then it penetrates a little deeper into the substratum, beyond the reach of our unaided senses.

At the same time Patanjali rejects the outlook of what is usually called idealism, which I prefer to call ideaism, namely, the belief that there is no real object there, but that our world is only a collection of ideas or thoughts existing in our consciousness, and would at once disappear if our thought-activity ceased. He does not object, however, to the belief that thought has power in molding forms; we have, in fact, the whole theory of the psychic powers to support this. But all such forms are held to partake of the nature of the world-substratum, which always shows itself in matter (or resistivity), energy and law,[1] called by him the three fundamental Qualities of the world.

IV, 15. "From the difference of minds in regarding the same object (we infer) the different ways of the two (that is, mind and the world)."

This is another way of saying that mind and object are different in nature, from which we must conclude that objects are not merely things in the mind. Several persons can look at the same object and see it differently, according to their own predilections. The inability of witnesses to agree as to fact is seen every day in law courts. Therefore the object is something outside those minds.

In the next aphorism Patanjali challenges the doubter of the objective reality of objects with a rhetorical question:

IV, 16. "And if an object depending on one mind were (at some time) not cognized by it, would it then exist?"

Patanjali presumes the answer to this to be "No." If it be held that an object exists solely because it is being thought into view by somebody, it would be reasonable to assume that in the absence of that thought this object would cease to be. Besides, it has been said, many things would then have only fronts, without backs or insides. It is known, however, with regard to any object, that many minds can see it, and also that the mind which saw it yesterday can see it again today. So the theory that objects are merely things being thought by minds will not do. In our modern day we can go further in this test of objectivity; we can leave an object in a dark room with a camera turned towards it and a flashlight timed to go off in the absence of any person, and afterward develop the photograph of the object standing there. Another very simple indication of the reality of a solid object lies in the fact that

---

[1] This triplicity also appears again in our ideas of space, time and order or constant relation.

you can stumble over a heap of rubbish when walking in the dark.

IV, 17. "An object can be known or unknown to the mind, because of its requiring to be colored by it."

If a thing is to be a known thing it must color a mind. But it can be "there" without coloring a mind, in which case it would be an unknown thing for the time being.

The mind is all-pervading, say some Hindu philosophers. They mean that it is not limited or qualified by material boundaries, as physical objects are. It pervades all objects to which it turns its attention, and in this process meets with no material obstruction.

The function of thought operates from centers within itself. Its space is time, for every act of thought takes time. It is the mind that converts a succession of material noises into music by holding a sheaf of them in its time-hand. It looks to the past and the future and does not know the pure present, which is as much a mystery as its two partners, past and future. The present aphorism reminds us that while all objects are knowable, no object is actually known until it is admitted and received into the mind which, to use Patanjali's term, is then colored by it. We may notice, in passing, that the mind with its five sense-organs and its five action-organs[1] constitutes a focusing instrument, and is itself known by what in modern terminology is called self-consciousness. This does not mean that it is conscious of itself. It builds a false self onto its consciousness, as we have seen when studying aphorism II, 6 in Chapter 5.

Consciousness arises because the mind is not only subject to influence from objects or from without, but also to another influence—from the real man, from within. From without it

[1] The five sense-organs are for hearing, touch, sight, taste and smell, in which the law or order or rhythm quality predominates. The five action-organs are of speech, handling, walking, excretion and generation, in which the energy quality predominates.

receives the reflections of objects; from within, the reflection
of the consciousness of the real man. It is only the false self
that can be known by the mind when it is colored by that
idea. We are quite often conscious without remembering ourselves.

IV, 18. "*The ideas in the mind are always known to its owner,
the real man, because he is without transformations.*"

If the man were not unchangeable, as he is, he would know
the contents of the mind at some times and not at other times,
or he would know some part of the contents of the mind and
not some other part. But if we say that pure consciousness is
the real man—that the real man *is* consciousness, not *has* consciousness—we must then infer that he is not subject to transformation, but always knows the reflections in the mind. That
the mind, on the other hand, is not itself conscious is strongly
affirmed by Patanjali in his next aphorism:

IV, 19. "*It (the mind) is not self-illuminate, on account of its
perceptibility.*"

Light and the eye are not conscious, but they are objects
of consciousness. So also the brain. In our study of Withdrawal, in Chapter 8, we have seen that the physical operations of the sense-organs can and often do proceed without
any response in consciousness. It is now stated that the mind,
like a camera receiving pictures in itself, is still within the
same category. It is itself an object, an instrument in the
series, without any light of consciousness of its own. Someone
must bring the light of consciousness into that camera, so that
the pictures in there may be seen. That someone is the owner,
the real man. As Patanjali's philosophy adheres firmly to the
proposition that seer and seen can never be the same, the seer
in this case cannot have the quality of perceptibility, which
belongs to the mind and its ideas, as well as to what we call
the "outer" world.

IV, 20. "Further, there is no knowledge of both at one time."

The seer and the seen cannot jointly be the object of sight to another seer. However much we may look into the mind of another person, we can never see his consciousness as an object, and however closely we may examine our own minds the same is true.

A person may say to himself, "I am conscious of my thought of a cow and also of my consciousness of it at the same time." Yes, he is conscious of three things at once—the cow, the thought of the cow, and the false self—all objects. Your knowledge of your consciousness is of an idea of consciousness in the mind; it is not the pure consciousness of the real man. Now somebody may suggest, Patanjali thinks, that each of us has two minds, one of which cognizes the other, so he says:

IV, 21. "In perceptibility (of the mind) by another mind, there would be excess of cognition, and confusion of memories."

If we posit or imagine a dual mind within us, one watching the other, it would be necessary for our second mind to be observed by a third, our third by a fourth and so on without end. Each being an object in turn, consciousness would recede to infinity.

With this aphorism, Patanjali completes his argument for the existence of the unchanging real man which he began in IV, 18. He next describes the relations between the real man and the mind, and the way in which the mind and the world come to the end of their work for the real man, who then achieves his complete Independence.

IV, 22. "Consciousness knows its own higher mind—though it does not move in connection (with anything)—by the arising of its image."

The important point here is that the mind receives reflections from the world of objects on one hand, and from the pure consciousness of the unchanging real man on the other. This produces two aspects of the mind, which we may for convenience call lower and higher, or mind colored by ideas and mind colored by the real man. So the mind partakes of the character of both the world and the real man. Consciousness is not merely knowing; it is feeling also, and will. These are governing powers among objects.

The practice of yoga thus becomes a contest between the lower mind and the higher mind, for while the lower collects experiences which in the earlier stages keep the mind in bondage to the world (through the Sources of Trouble), the higher mind gradually asserts the enjoyment of pure consciousness, governing the ideas in the mind and through them the objects in the world. The yogī lives in the higher mind, which by gradually asserting its government and fulfilling its interest in the real man, completes the light of knowledge and in the end releases the real man, as we shall see. Consciousness does not know itself as an object; but knows the higher mind as an object—and therefore as not itself—when its image arises.

IV, 23. *"The mind being colored by (both) the Looker and the seen, has everything within its scope."*

In the yoga philosophy the standpoint of the student is practical. He starts his thinking and his work from what he knows and where he is. It seems to him that, as a Western philosopher once put it, he is on a ladder, and he can see the rungs above him and the rungs below him, both going out of sight. He finds himself in this dual mind, and decides to proceed on the side of law and order, love and thought, which are coordinating and unifying powers. He is able to see that his idea of himself is full of errors and is possibly fundamentally erroneous, but he does not make the mistake of trying to set aside or to destroy this defective self. He prefers to work for the perfection or fulfillment of those parts of his experience which belong to the reflection in him of the real man. He finds that this leads to achievement and success in material life as well as in the mind. He finds, in fact, that the correct treatment of things, persons and thoughts is also the correct treatment of himself, and that life is thus so coherent that living, not retreat, is the road to his own final integrity and fulfillment.

Treatments of yoga not agreeing with this principle, which we sometimes come across, are corruptions of yoga, based upon wrong ideas. To torture the body, flout the human emotions and shrink from life through either pride or fear—all are within the category of superstition or substitution of error for truth.

The mind exists to some purpose. It is obviously an instrument. The would-be yogī decides to use it, which means in his present condition, to use himself, for the attainment of the full height of man. He does not know what the real man is: he will not attempt to define that real man, but he decides to fare forth on that voyage of discovery into the land of truth which is mysteriously hidden in every common thing of life, wherein lies the nourishment of his very soul.

IV, 24. *"Also, the mind, with all its innumerable latencies, exists for the sake of another, for it works by combination (with the real man)."*

Further examination shows that as the mind thus fares forth, it has no purpose of its own, but is, as it were, a living storehouse of things collected and kept for someone else. It collects experiences of objects, keeps them in memory and compares and combines them. It can bring together pictures of things not connected in time and space, and from the composition it produces ideas and plans. Often, having rearranged the pictures before the mind's eye, it can work to alter and rearrange the things from which its pictures were originally derived. As a result of all this activity it is full of latencies, from which arise new paths of experience—the avoidance of that, the seeking of this—all the company of good and bad with their pleasures and pains, actual and imaginary. Thus it runs on aimlessly, except when called to order by the aspirant who wishes to bring purpose or at least method into his life. It exists for another, the real man. It is to be more and more his instrument, his tool, his machine, in the world.

The mind is always serving the man, because it produces a kind of yoga in action, even when there is no knowledge or intention of such a thing. We have seen in our study of Concentration, Meditation and Contemplation in an earlier chapter that our life is enhanced by that process. I mean that after a Mind-poise we are more alive than we were before, if we have practiced it sincerely. Perception, observation, thinking, have more color than before; action has clearer purpose; work greater efficiency.

I want now to say that the mind by its impulses from its latencies leads to a process in the outer world similar to that produced by Concentration, etc. in the mind itself. Impelled by some desire rising from some impression, a man decides, let us say, to work in the garden. He wants to see some nice flowers, bushes and perhaps trees, agreeably arranged about a lawn. He sets to work, thinks and plans, studies his landscape, soils, fertilizers, and seasonable plants. He digs, and weeds, and plants, and breathes deeply of the pure air of the out-of-doors. He benefits in body and mind.

First, be it noted, the latency awakens a desire and produces interest, which at once leads to a kind of concentration. Instead of attending vaguely to a great number and variety of indefinite thoughts and things, the man narrows the field of his interest and focuses his attention on this one idea of making a garden. Secondly, all his thinking and planning and study form a kind of meditation or expansion of thought within that limited field, where idea and purpose are clear and strong. And thirdly, in the course of his work many occasions arise for some simple and perhaps quite unintentional contemplation, and pleasant reflections ensue which the man does not attribute to intuition, though they often are that. See, too, how all the work done in the garden has impermanent effects, but the good done to the man is permanent, an increase of his powers and his life. This alone is evidence that the mind exists for the sake of the man, not for itself.

We now begin to consider the thoughts of a yogī well established in the higher mind and intellectually aware of the distinction between mind and man.

IV, 25. *"On the part of him who sees the distinction (between mind and real man), there is a turning away from thoughts about the nature of self."*

Before reaching the conclusion that the real man cannot be defined or thought of in terms of any of the objects or categories of the world or of the mind itself, it is a useful part of practical philosophy to think upon the nature of self. "Who and what am I?" comes in as part of the self-study recommended to the beginner in yoga.

There are very useful meditations in this field, in which you look at things and try and see yourself there. Look at your fingers meditatively, until you find yourself feeling, "Such queer things cannot be I." This is not the same as to make the intellectual statement: "Objects and self cannot be in the same category." Pause and reflect that that statement itself is an idea in the category of objects, and does not inform us about the self.

After the fingers, you can take other parts of the body, and finally the whole body. Look into your own eyes in a mirror. Don't hurry—don't think of time—and don't be intellectual. Ponder on your personality, its world, the world. This practice of Mind-poise will bring its own experience, beginning with a refutation of the ideas, "I am this—or this," and ending with intuitive experience of the distinction between the mind and the real man. The Sources of Trouble will become not merely weakened, but faded almost to the point of disappearance. That old self of yours will no longer be so interesting.

IV, 26. *Then the mind is deep in Discrimination and mainly pointed to Independence."*

IV, 27. *"At intervals there are other thoughts, arising from the habit-molds."*

IV, 28. *"The abandoning of those is like that of the Sources of Trouble, as already described."*

We move swiftly now, in our review of the last phases of bondage.

IV, 29. *"In the case of one having no interest of any kind even in intellection, on account of Discrimination-knowledge, there is the Contemplation called 'cloud of rectitude.'"*

This means that the yogī at this stage does not expect intellectual activity to give him the knowledge that he wants of the self or real man. His mind is constantly discriminating the distinction of the real man from both object and mind. The contemplation which he pursues is therefore not any of those leading to psychic powers which we have already reviewed, but is this one called "cloud of rectitude." This name calls for explanation.

First of all, a cloud is not thought about in India as in America. When the villagers in India see the dark and heavy rain cloud approaching after a long season of dryness and brassy skies, they rejoice exceedingly. They imagine with great pleasure how it will soon be sprinkling the thirsty earth with precious water. For this reason they go so far as to picture the incarnation of God in His aspect of the Preserver as deep blue in color, and they call him Krishna, which means "dark." He is the divine incarnation who gives the spiritual teaching in the world-famous poem entitled "The Bhagavad Gita" or "Song of the Lord." So much for the "cloud" part of "cloud of rectitude."

Now as to "rectitude." The original word is *dharma*. That is a noun derived from a verbal root which means to uphold, maintain, support or sustain. In human conduct *dharma* is therefore used for the prescribed social proprieties, such as crossing the city street when the green light shines and not against the red, wearing correct clothing, pursuing a suitable livelihood honestly, and, in its perfection, loving your neighbor as yourself. In olden days in India orthodox people read into *dharma* the idea of obedience to rules of caste, such as that of following your father's profession or occupation and marrying within your social group—rules now rapidly losing their hold on the people.

There is self-regarding *dharma* also. This means that a man is true to himself when he maintains his own integrity and faculties. This I have called obedience to spiritual laws, which operate within the mind, not by external injunctions and compulsions. This is "the living law of the higher self." It does not go against obedience to external rules and regulations which the man thinks it right to obey, but it inculcates the rectitude of disobedience when truth to oneself requires it. Primarily, then, a man must maintain his powers, which all come within the triple classification of action, love and thought. A man, if true to himself, must act, and do so with love and thought. This simple formula provides for all the virtues, and, negatively, indicates that all vices are included within idleness, selfishness and thoughtlessness.

Remember, our yogī is still living in the world. His habitual thoughts and his meditations are upon rectitude. His actions will follow these. He is now in a position to derive the greatest living quality or reality from every experience, because he brings to bear upon it the whole light and power of all his faculties. But he is not ruled by externals, blown hither and thither by every wind—driven by circumstances, ruled by self-personality, or drifting on the current of an uncontrolled mind. In brief, he is not a slave of Nature. He will treat all circumstances, including persons and things, with respect, allotting to them the integrity which he claims for himself, and giving them his action, love and thought, but will not be fascinated nor driven by any of them. He lives in the world as a "cloud of rectitude," and he is very near to freedom.

IV, 30. "From that follows the retirement of Sources of Trouble and karmas."

IV, 31. "Then, in the case of him who is free from all coverings and impurities, what-is-to-be-known becomes small, on account of the infinity of (his) knowledge.

IV, 32. "And from that comes the end of the succession of transformations of the Qualities, which have finished their work."

The Sources of Trouble, as we have seen in an earlier chapter, give rise to karmas, including body (i.e. birth), life-state and the rest. The conditions so produced are real. They are also educative. Every man coming into the world has some things which are to-be-known. He needs not to know everything. Everything is everybody's business, but something is one man's and from it he will obtain his fruit of experience. As I remarked in an earlier chapter, to learn to play the violin you require one violin, not a million, not even two. To awaken love in me I needed one mother—I need not be born from every mother in the world. What I need to know or realize I can learn from my own karmas, which constitute "my world," which is my piece of *the* world. With the capacity you acquired in learning to play on one violin you can play if needed on other violins. The love which I have learned through one mother can arise towards other people. Thus faculty acquired from finite things is infinite in itself.

Another point: When I have awakened my faculties with the aid of particular karmic experiences, I do not need and indeed do not want them any more. The other day I overheard a conversation between a furniture dealer and a housewife. She was expressing doubt whether to sell two lamps. The dealer asked: "How long have you had those lamps?" The lady replied, "Oh, about six years." "Surely," said the man, with great decision, "you wouldn't want to be looking at anything longer than that, would you?"

I recall another incident, also within my own experience, which illustrates the same point. A teacher of painting was taking some of his pupils into a forest. They came to their usual clearing. The teacher said to one of them, "What will you paint today?" The pupil indicated a particular tree. "But," exclaimed the teacher, "you have already painted that a number of times." "Yes," replied the pupil, "but I haven't got it right yet." When he got it right, that is, when he had derived all he could from that experience, he would be satisfied with that, and to paint it again would be a bore.

The most striking example, however, of this principle occurs in connection with jokes. I tell you one today and you laugh heartily. I tell it to you again tomorrow and you smile politely, and with a little pleasurable reminiscence perhaps. The next time we meet, I begin it again, but it is no longer a joke.

We cannot, of course, prescribe for a particular person how long the enjoyment of a thing will last. Shallow minds soon tire of a thing and must have novelty, but they come round again and again to the same things. Deeper minds may often take longer to derive full benefit from an object, but more often than others they complete the work.

The general theory for our present purpose is that the mind

comes to an end of its education when it is so full of understanding that the covering of light is entirely destroyed and
its only pleasure now is in the reflection of the real man in itself. The yogī now becomes independent in the midst of all,
for nothing is happening contrary to his will and pleasure.
But in that case, anyhow, the objects of experience, composed
of the Qualities of Nature, have finished their work for him.
Having no Sources of Trouble and so making no new karmas,
he is now free from the Qualities. If he desires to return to
birth he can, but he has nothing to gain for himself, and if he
chooses he can retire from it all and live the true life of the
real man, free from the obstructions of this world. The statement that the Qualities have finished their work needs the
addition of the two words "for him."

Patanjali now feels it necessary to elucidate "the succession
of transformations," and does so in a further aphorism:

IV, 33. *"Succession, which is the counter-correlative of a moment, is to be given up at the end of the last transformation."*

Of all the aphorisms in this book this is probably the most
difficult to translate into English, although it must be said that
its general purport is very clear and easy to grasp, namely,
that there is a last transformation, as far as the yogī is concerned.

Patanjali's difficulty appears to be that he does not want to
suppose that abstract change is a reality, but has all along
been thinking of a succession of transformations, so that at
one moment an object appears in a certain condition and a
moment later it appears somewhat different. In this way,
what is now a new cloth later on comes to be an old cloth.
These transformations are considered as jumps, like the pictures in a cinematograph film, and they are due to actions
which imply contacts and disjunctions of objects, actions remaining a mystery. So they appeared to one of the ancients,

who said: "A thing cannot move, because it cannot move in the place where it is and it cannot move in the place where it isn't." To this, moderns would rejoin, "But it can move *from* the place where it is *to* the place where it isn't." Observe then, I would comment, that "from" and "to" represent a deep truth, to which this place and that place are but ancillary truths. The static is not the fundamental; we know nothing static, and what we call the present moment is gone even before we can announce that it has arrived.

To Patanjali a transformation is a static thing existing for a moment. We have been thinking of transformations as static in such moments, and now we need to see that the fact called succession is not itself a transformation. So we define it by saying it is the counter-correlative of a moment. The technicality here is that we can define a moment of time as that which has the absence of succession. It is just as if we said, "On this table there is no jar," in that case the jar is the counter-correlative of the mentioned absence. So a moment is that which has succession for its counter-correlative. And then we can define succession as the counter-correlative of a moment. Thus we have established an epistemological relation between a static transformation and a succession, and we know exactly what we mean when we speak of succession.

Now comes the end of worldly life and the beginning of free life. Patanjali's next aphorism describes it from both points of view:

IV, 34. "Independence is the counter-product when the Qualities of Nature are devoid of purpose for the real man, or, the power of consciousness stands firm in its own nature."

CHAPTER 17

THE TWO KINDS OF CONTEMPLATION

Having studied the theory of yoga to the very end, at which Independence is reached and there is that self-realization which is spoken of as perfect knowledge of the real man by himself, we must turn again to the practice. For this purpose I have reserved a portion of Patanjali's teaching given in his First Section. In that portion Patanjali gave the beginner a preview of the advanced modes of Contemplation that the yogī will take up after achieving the power of Contemplation. In his Second Section the teacher entered upon his instructions regarding the practices for developing that power. I have rearranged the order in this respect to suit the modern mind and world.

Let us first recall the nature of Contemplation. It is full mental activity without (1) the mind-wandering which is natural (or habitual) to the ideas in the mind; and (2) the process of thinking which is concerned in knowing the object of thought better than before. This is the same as to say: "Full mental activity preceded by Concentration and Meditation and their cessation." Such Contemplation can follow upon perception of any object or thought. Also, it can be involuntary as well as voluntary. In ordinary life it occurs quite frequently, involuntarily. In the practice of yoga it is voluntary. Let us also recall that a given Contemplation is within the sphere of the object of Concentration and Meditation which preceded it. The full mental activity—which is Contemplation—does not, as it were, float off into space.

When I say Contemplation is full mental activity, I think

211

most readers of these words will recognize it as within their own experience, perhaps when looking at a beautiful sunset or coming upon a grand view of a range of mountains, perhaps in reading a poem or looking at a picture, perhaps when introduced to a new and illuminating idea in natural or social science or philosophy. Perhaps they will have felt the hurt, too, when somebody present blurts out, "Oh, look, how lovely, just like the picture in mother's dining room," or, seeing a far-away look in your eyes, someone suddenly demands to know what you are thinking about, and thus jolts you back from your unself-conscious contemplation into meditation, or knowledge-thought. It is not, I hasten to add, that the fruit of Contemplation is not knowledge. It is that. When Contemplation naturally ends, you bring that back with you to your ordinary mental state, where it illumines a whole field of thought. It is understanding and insight, and it proves its worth in every sphere of science, philosophy, religion, art and practical life.

Contemplations may be divided into two classes: (1) with cognition of an object; and (2) without cognition of an object. The former may again be divided into two groups: (1) with a concrete object; and (2) with an abstract object.

I, 17. "It (i.e. Contemplation) is cognitive when accompanied by forms of inspection, investigation, delight, or sense of power."

This calls for considerable explanation. If your object is concrete, your Concentration will pass into Meditation on the lines of inspection, physical (by observation) and mental (by reasoning, including comparing it with other things). If it is not within your own sense experience, but something you have been told about by somebody else, your process will begin with taking careful notice of the words, so as to get them right, and then going on to their meaning (which is conventional, as given in a reliable dictionary, of course) and the object-knowledge carried in that meaning.

If your object is abstract, your Concentration will pass into Meditation on the line of mental investigation. Without that kind of deliberation or discussion or reasoning and judgment, your object will lack point and clearness. I am here using the term abstract very freely, to include all objects beyond the range of the senses, as well as truly abstract ideas. Take, for example, the chemical atom; we can smell, taste and feel various chemicals, but the atom is a mental conception, though corresponding to a reality of which we have indirect or inferential evidence. Space, time, motion and many others are within this group. In it, also, are the true abstract ideas, such as "cowness" possessed by all cows in all their varieties, qualities like weight and goodness, and all the operations of the mind itself. The term subtle is usually applied to things too fine or small to be within the reach of the senses but conceivable in the mind as actual or real. The class of abstract things or ideas includes everything of this kind that is verbally definable.

Notice that in the explanation just given I have referred only to the mental part of the mind, but we have in the mind also conscious experiences composed of feelings and the sense of power or will. Incidentally, it will be noticed that all three varieties of mental experience are related to the five Sources of Trouble—knowledge to Ignorance, feelings to Desire, Aversion and Possessiveness, and sense of power to Self-personality. Remember, too, that Mind-poise is always practiced on pleasurable things; we do not dwell on the unpleasant, as will be seen in aphorism I, 33, which will be dealt with in this chapter in due course. People who do not know about the effects of thought dwell upon evils, sorrows, sins and horrors, but in yoga this simply is not done. It is undesirable and dangerous. Therefore, if and insofar as your Meditation is emotional, it is described as with delight, and if and insofar as it has to do with the will it brings a sense of power.

I, 18. *"The other (Contemplation), with only habit-molds for its residue, follows upon practice on the mental image of stoppage."*

In this case the Mind-poise will begin without any objective idea, but with the idea of giving up all of them. The ability to dwell on that conception depends upon the development of the higher Uncoloredness which, as we have seen in Chapter 3, is characterized not merely by the idea of "enough," but with a conceptual vision of the existence of the real man in the higher mind, which has become pure law unstained by obstructions in the form of desire for materiality or energy.

The practice of this form of Contemplation puts a complete end to the Sources of Trouble, which have already been weakened. In this case there is nothing in the mind that can produce objective karmas, so only the old habit-molds remain after it is over, without any new additions. But before full attainment, the conception of the real man may be tainted by ideas of and desires for spiritual states of being. One may give up the idea of and longing for objective existence but still cling to the notion of pure existence in the powers of the higher mind—the mind by itself, life standing in its own power and living in its own light.

We must not mistake the non-cognitive Contemplation for Independence itself. There are attainments in this Contemplation which give long life in the purest form of external existence—bodiless enjoyment of the sense of power and delight for long periods of time. These attainments the true yogī avoids, so as to achieve full Independence. Patanjali says:

I, 19. *"There is the thought of existence in the case of the bodiless beings and those who are absorbed in Nature."*

Not wanting the bodily state, but deeply devoted to the idea of some kind of bodiless life, or to life bathed, as it were, in some element of Nature such as fire, these people obtain what they want and enjoy it for long periods until their desire and devotion wear themselves out. The Hindus have an idea of what is called a *deva* state of existence, which involves pleasures and powers limited only by mental conceptions. The yogī may find this enjoyment so tempting that he yields to it, in which case he ceases for the time his final yoga effort. But others are not tempted aside by these grand accomplishments; they remain yogīs and pursue their purpose to the very end of Independence, to be reached through a realization of the distinction between the real man and all mental existence. Do not, however, read any disparagement into the pursuit of bodiless life as a goal. Every person is at liberty to stop at any wayside inn for a rest or to please himself.

This bodiless state is often considered to be related to the idea of periods in "heaven" (*swarga*) between death and rebirth, which, it is held, sometimes become very long, lasting until the superphysical desires are exhausted and a new impulse for the definiteness of the physical state begins.

I, 20. "In the case of others, it is preceded by faith, vigor, memory, Contemplation and understanding."

These things are taken successively. Faith, or confidence in the general idea and teaching of yoga, gives rise to a vigorous pursuit of yoga practice according to the instructions here given. Memory then comes in constantly—because the yogī is vigorously interested, so that he does not forget and neglect his purpose at any time. Cognitive Contemplation then carries him on to an understanding of his goal. That understanding, with all the rest of this series backing it up, will save him from glorious temptations and bring him safely to the Discrimination, which will at last enable him to complete his realization of Independence.

The source and foundation of success in yoga, not only in the non-cognitive Contemplation, but also in the earlier stages—including the cognitive Contemplation and all the paranormal faculties and powers which it can be used to procure, is faith. It arises and grows by experience. A little experience of even a small intuition—the strength that it gives in daily living in the world, the delight it infuses into the feelings, the illumination of the mind—gives faith a good start, and it grows from strength to strength by continued experience.

Trust grows and it is essential to progress and impetus. Its chief characteristics, I would say, are an absence of fear and prejudice.

Have I defined it negatively? Yes, because this faith is natural to us, not procured and attached, and it shines when a little experience of its good removes fear. I could give dozens of illustrations of this. Suppose you obtain a piece of intuitive knowledge by mental clairvoyance—you want it to be confirmed, so through fear you interpose from below the idea that it was given to you as a boon or a blessing by a Great Siddha or Adept or Master, or perhaps through prejudice you translate it into words or colors or other symbols or similitudes of your familiar world, thinking thereby to give it more reality. This does not block you entirely, but it introduces obstructions—many pitfalls for the unwary. Faith, however, quickly overcomes all obstacles. Patanjali will mention these obstacles, but he tells us now of its power in leading to the non-cognitive Contemplation.

I, 21. "It (i.e. the non-cognitive Contemplation) is near for those whose impetus is intense."

I, 22. "Even in this a distinction of mild, medium and highest measure (may be seen)."

The reader may very reasonably ask why faith has been brought up in this advanced stage and not before. The answer is that faith cannot be expected to be genuine and powerful in the early stages, as it depends upon some experience.

Another question that arises is: Is there any other thing that will help, along with or instead of, faith? The teacher says:

I, 23. "Or, it (i.e. the non-cognitive Contemplation) comes from Attentiveness to God."

We have already had Attentiveness to God as one of the first three practices, explained in Chapter 4. People may say that the expression "Attentiveness to God" is very mild and does not convey a sense of devotion and dependence, or prostration before an overwhelmingly superior being. Really, Attentiveness to God means more than devotion and prostration, because it must accompany a feeling of the omnipresence or the absolute presence of God. I must now give a full translation of the aphorisms on this subject, as I merely referred to them in Chapter 4.

I, 24. "God is a particular soul, unaffected by containers of Sources of Trouble, works and (their) fruition."

I, 25. "In Him is the unexcelled source of all knowledge."

I, 26. "He was the teacher also of the ancients, because He is not limited by time."

I, 27. "His indicator is the sacred word."

I, 28. "(There should be) repetition of it, with thought upon its meaning."

Now we come to the importance of the whole matter, when Patanjali says in his concluding aphorism on the subject of God:

I, 29. "From this there is understanding of the individual consciousness, also an absence of obstacles."

This is the advanced teaching about God. From Attentiveness to God you know yourself, because you, as real man, are what He is. Do not discourage devotion; believe and feel that you are enveloped in all good by Him, that He is the knower of everything and the supreme teacher—and then, at last, know that "Thou art That." It is the Vedantins who constantly revert to the Upanishadic teaching: "Thou art That," but Patanjali here announces the same truth in other words. He makes us understand that it does not mean "This thou of thee is That," but "What That is, thou art." Learn this truth by yoga, not as a statement of becoming, but of being, not as a development, evolution, achievement or attainment, but, as I have frequently pointed out before in this book, a remover of obstacles, an uncovering of the light.

It is well known that the Sānkhya philosophy of old India does not include a God who runs a school for our benefit. Buddhism took up the same belief. The non-dual Vedantism of Shankarāchārya has the same view. But Patanjali admitted the idea of God for purposes of understanding oneself, and Shankarāchārya also admitted it in the form of what was called Shabda Brahman (as already mentioned) for the purposes of Concentration and Meditation and as a prelude to "Thou art That," but affirmed also "Not This; Not This," including all that can be conceived of Brahman in terms of mind and personal knowledge.

There is logic and consistency in the karma theory, if man causes all his own experience, if it is a form of extuition or self-education which man prescribes for himself, if it all occurs within his own volition and acceptance, and if the incidence of it at any time is also willed in the depth or heart of his own being. This man, then, is surely godlike, so the conception of God can be encouraged as a means to self-realization. The Sānkhya and Yoga philosophies allow the thought of many individual real men or souls. They do not affirm it as a fact knowable to the mind. The number 1 (one) does not differ in Nature from the other digits, and is not to be attributed to that real man which cannot be compassed by limited experience or any thought of the mind.

The teacher now goes on to describe the obstacles which the advanced student can avoid by an understanding of his own divinity.

I, 30. *"Disease, dullness, indecision, carelessness, sloth, worldliness, mistaken views, losing the way and instability— these splurgings of the mind are obstacles."*

I, 31. *"Co-existing with these splurgings are distress, despair, nervousness and disordered inbreathing and outbreathing."*

I, 32. *"For the purpose of preventing these, there should be practice of the one truth."*

We may repeat the one and constant lesson: realization of the real man must be sought; all else belongs to the realm of the Sources of Trouble. This is not to be merely a philosophic realization through thought. Actions and feelings cannot be ignored. Every detail of daily life contains the infinite and supreme lesson when the eye sees the truth, and this makes Independence, or freedom, not a matter of escape but of realization in the midst of all the people and things of "my world." This is a matter for the pure mind. Remember that ideas are matter in the mind, Sources of Trouble are energy in the mind, but light or clearness is the law of the mind. When ideas and Sources of Trouble are silent, the mind is pure. Patanjali says:

I, 33. *"From the habitual mood of friendliness, sympathy, gladness and disregard respectively towards those who are happy, suffering, good and bad, comes purity of mind."*

It is implied that this is another way of dealing with the obstacles, or rather that the obstacles will not arise if this mood of the mind is constant. The word which I have translated "habitual mood" includes feeling as well as thought, and also implies a kind of pondering or quiet activity.

Simple as this aphorism sounds, it is of the deepest significance, for it goes to the very root of the matter. For ordinary persons without any great ambitions towards spiritual or material perfection, it points out the law of happiness and success.

What will it mean if I see a rich man happily driving his car while I am toilfully walking in the dust and hoping for a "lift"? That I shall have a happy moment in seeing him happy. But more than that, there will be results all through my body; my step will be more springy, my breathing will be deeper, my eye will see more brightly, and my whole nature will be more attuned to positive living, so that when I reach my goal my business will be done cheerfully, confidently and well, and the persons whom I then meet will be glad that they have met me.

There will not, in fact, be much more of that trudging in the dust, for this is the way of success when the mood is genuine and complete. But if the thought is just a pretense or a trick, with an eye to material profit by it, the results will be quite different, in mind and body and outer life.

To the yogī, with his developing powers of mind, the importance of this aphorism is even greater. It would be positively dangerous for him to dwell upon evils or harbor an unkind thought.

I, 34. "Or (the obstacles can be reduced) by throwing out and holding of the breath."

This word "or" is not to be understood as an alternative. I would like to translate it as, "Another useful matter, but optional, is . . ." This rather long expression best represents the thought and intention of the original.

In this place Patanjali does not use words that mean regulation of the breath. He is thinking of clearing out the lungs, which should be fully emptied, at least occasionally, of spent air, impure gases, smoke and dust. But see also the subject matter of regulation of the breath in my Chapter 8.

I, 35. *"Another thing: The rise of oncoming sensitivity causes mental steadiness."*

I, 36. *"Also: (The rise of the) peaceful inner light (causes mental steadiness)."*

I, 37. *"Again: The mind regarding those free from Desire (will be steady)."*

I, 38. *"Or: Dwelling upon knowledge of dream and sleep (conduces to steadiness)."*

I, 39. *"Another way: From meditation upon whatever you are specially interested in (comes mental steadiness)."*

I, 40. *"Its mastery extends from the smallest to the greatest (things)."*

The point of this group of recommendations is to establish a center in the mind in which to see things clearly and see them whole—a place of calmness and freedom from jostling. I have likened this to a telephone booth in a railway station or a drug store—you go inside and shut the door and suddenly there is quiet.

It is not difficult to establish your mental telephone booth by any of these means and a modicum of imagination and will power, and then to retire into it whenever you wish and afterward emerge from it refreshed and stronger to deal with all the distractions that may come. It is not a retreat from life, but a means of gathering yourself and your forces together, analogous to a short period of good bodily relaxation, in which you stop your physical activities for a little while but come out of it with your body more coordinated and able to recover all the supposedly lost time by much superior work.

In your telephone booth or, as a Hindu would think of it,

in the shining lotus-flower within the heart, you may dwell for a while upon the inner peace, or upon the thought of some great Personage free from Desire, or upon the states of dream and sleep, in both of which the mind is not driven by outside things, or in fact upon anything you specially like. As a very small boy, I remember, I got great release from worry by going into imaginary toyshops—there were caverns after caverns underground filled with the most fascinating things arranged on platforms on each side, where I would quietly walk along and linger to inspect one thing after another. While writing this I am also reminded of a Chinese doctor I once knew who habitually employed a part of his leisure in sitting and imagining he was in heaven; he told me he thought it must be almost as good as the real thing!

You may have a fad which is a harmless thing but quite impracticable. Do not rebuke yourself on that account and drive it away, calling it foolish or trivial. Use it for mental relaxation and for going to sleep. As long as you know what you are doing, it can do no harm.

One method for such retirement is that mentioned in I, 35, in which the aspirant listens to the sounds going on in the body, or becomes intent upon scents, or inner lights. These may lead on to the faculties of clairvoyance etc., but that is not what is being considered here. However, having brought up the subject of developing paranormal senses in your quietude, I must add one word of advice. Subject them to occasional tests, if they have reference to physical things. I know perfectly well how tender and delicate these new sprouts are, and I would not on any account wither them away in their infancy by subjection to the harsh judgment and criticism which are necessary in the affairs of ordinary active life. But remember another thing with which to balance this leniency. They are apt suddenly to flame into a great riot of growth, dazzlingly attractive, but for the most part a product of imagination and that unconscious propagation of ideas which we commonly experience in a very mild form in what we call mind-wandering.

Now, back to our telephone booth. When the mind frees itself from the obstacles mentioned in I, 30, it becomes an accurate reflector of what comes into it from the outer world through the senses and from the real man within.

I have spoken of the world as composed of matter, energy and law, and have said that the mind also is of that world. The mind, when not distracted or impeded, is law in the world. Do not human beings carry with them law and order, and, where they dwell, convert jungles into gardens? The obstructions of matter, the exuberances of energy are mastered and used by the successful mind, and do not disturb or cloud its pure workings, so much so that quite often the word for law, order or rhythm is used to indicate the pure mind itself.

This brings us all the way back to the beginning of our study, where we learned that yoga is control of the ideas in the mind. If at any moment the existing ideas are kept quiet the perceptions will become clear and true. The effects of this may be treated as another chapter.

CHAPTER 18

THE DUSTLESS MIRROR

Patanjali says:

I, 41. "Correct imagery is the reception of anything that is within the classes of knower, knowing or known, when the ideas have declined—like the action of a flawless gem."

We have come to a vital point in our argument and yoga practice. To be able to be so free from prejudices, likes, dislikes, fears, angers, hopes and all the Sources of Trouble and Ideas that we can see something as it really presents itself, is a great achievement. In my account of some experiments in thought transference, I have given some illustrations of what usually happens, when the ideas already in the mind affect incoming perceptions, as they usually do. But when those ideas are kept quiet for the time being, the mind can operate with correct imagery. The object so presented may be some object or idea external to the mind, or correct ideas with regard to the mind itself and its instruments of knowing, that is, the sense-organs and the mental processes of knowing. Some of these may be abstract ideas—it is not a matter of experience only through the senses. The main point is that the image shall not be modified from truth or tainted by any preconceived ideas. There is then simple witnessing of what is there and what is going on.

I, 42. "In that case, when there is a mixture of thoughts about word, meaning and knowledge, it is the correct imagery called inspectional."

Note what this means: Somebody tells us something—that is testimony; we consider the meaning of the words—that is inference; we then formulate a piece of the knowledge in the mind, which is correct if the testimony and inference are correct. For example, somebody says: "There is a dog in the garden"—we hear words, think of their meaning and form an idea. But if we saw the dog in the garden there would be no consideration of words and meanings, but only direct perception, without discussion.

I, 43. "*When memory is cleared away (and the mind) shines forth as the object alone, as though devoid of its own nature, it is non-inspectional.*"

Memory deals with the receipt of the information about the dog, and with the meaning of the words, and the setting up of the correct image, but when the image is established the words and meaning will be forgotten and the object alone will be in view. It will so occupy the mind that the latter will lose itself in the object on reaching full Contemplation.

I, 44. "*In the same way the investigational and the non-investigational, which have the subtle as their objects, are also explained.*"
I, 45. "*And that objectiveness of the subtle ends only at that which is beyond definition.*"

In Chapter 17 I have already described the four kinds of cognitive Contemplation. In connection with the fourth we must now observe that the subtle includes everything known or thinkable as far as the very root of matter, which is undefinable, being beyond form. Some may call the real man also subtle, but that is not correct, for he is not objective in any sense, and anything subtle is objective. It would be poor metaphysics to think that the infinite is nearer to the fine than to the dense, to the lighter than to the heavier, to the subtle than to the gross.

I, 46. "These (four) are only the Contemplation with seed."

Inasmuch as these forms of Contemplation are based upon external objects, they have reference to those, and the results in intuition or power return with the consciousness to the same point in the mind.

I, 47. "When there is full skill in the non-investigational Contemplation, there is the very pellucidity of the supreme self."

I, 48. "In that the cognition is full of truth."

I, 49. "Its objects are different from those of testamentary and inferential cognition, because its business is with particulars."

When we derive information from others it depends always upon some generalization and requires logic for its elucidation. When we are told that there is a dog in the garden, we have to think of dogs and "dogness" to get the idea of a dog there, and we have no perfectly clear idea of the particular dog. Even detailed description will not fully inform us, for each of the details leans upon a generality for its conveyance in words, and demands a further particularization in its genus, which again calls for more generalities, and so on without practical end. But if we have seen the particular dog, so accurately that we need not question ourselves as to whether it is really a dog or perhaps a fox or a wolf, there is nothing to be argued. It is direct perception, not inference, nor testimony. When the yogī is able thus to know directly the subtle objects of his Contemplation with perfect pellucidity, there is the highest poise and the very essence of true knowledge.

I, 50. "The habit-mold arising from that overcomes (all) other habit-molds."

This is similar to the habit of recall (in the practice of Concentration) used to overcome the previous habit of drifting.

I, 51. *"When there is control of that also, the seedless Contemplation arrives, because there is now the control of all."*

This seedless Contemplation is the non-cognitive Contemplation. How that leads on to Discrimination and Independence I have already explained in Chapter 17.

PATANJALI'S YOGA APHORISMS

APPENDIX I

PATANJALI'S YOGA APHORISMS

New Translation (1948) from Sanskrit into English

BY

PROFESSOR ERNEST EGERTON WOOD

Section I, On Contemplation

231

Section II, Description of the Practice

Section IV, On Independence

34. Independence is the counter-product when the Qualities of Nature are devoid of purpose for the real man, or, the power of consciousness stands firm in its own nature. 210

APPENDIX II

INDEX

Melvin Powers
SELF-IMPROVEMENT
LIBRARY

_____ABILITY TO LOVE Dr. Allan Fromme	$2.00
_____ACT YOUR WAY TO SUCCESSFUL LIVING Neil & Margaret Rau	2.00
_____ADVANCED TECHNIQUES OF HYPNOSIS Melvin Powers	1.00
_____ANIMAL HYPNOSIS Dr. F. A. Völgyesi	2.00
_____ASTROLOGY: A FASCINATING HISTORY P. Naylor	2.00
_____ASTROLOGY: HOW TO CHART YOUR HOROSCOPE Max Heindel	2.00
_____ASTROLOGY: YOUR PERSONAL SUN-SIGN GUIDE Beatrice Ryder	2.00
_____ASTROLOGY FOR EVERYDAY LIVING Janet Harris	2.00
_____ASTROLOGY GUIDE TO GOOD HEALTH Alexandra Kayhle	2.00
_____ASTROLOGY MADE EASY Astarte	2.00
_____ASTROLOGY MADE PRACTICAL Alexandra Kayhle	2.00
_____ASTROLOGY, ROMANCE, YOU AND THE STARS Anthony Novell	2.00
_____BEGINNER'S GUIDE TO WINNING CHESS Fred Reinfeld	2.00
_____BETTER CHESS — How to Play Fred Reinfeld	2.00
_____BICYCLING FOR FUN AND GOOD HEALTH Kenneth E. Luther	2.00
_____BOOK OF TALISMANS, AMULETS & ZODIACAL GEMS William Pavitt	3.00
_____BRIDGE BIDDING MADE EASY Edwin Kantar	5.00
_____BRIDGE CONVENTIONS Edwin Kantar	4.00
_____CHECKERS MADE EASY Tom Wiswell	2.00
_____CHESS IN TEN EASY LESSONS Larry Evans	2.00
_____CHESS MADE EASY Milton L. Hanauer	2.00
_____CHESS MASTERY — A New Approach Fred Reinfeld	2.00
_____CHESS PROBLEMS FOR BEGINNERS edited by Fred Reinfeld	2.00
_____CHESS SECRETS REVEALED Fred Reinfeld	2.00
_____CHESS STRATEGY — An Expert's Guide Fred Reinfeld	2.00
_____CHESS TACTICS FOR BEGINNERS edited by Fred Reinfeld	2.00
_____CHESS THEORY & PRACTICE Morry & Mitchell	2.00
_____CHILDBIRTH WITH HYPNOSIS William S. Kroger, M.D.	2.00
_____COIN COLLECTING FOR BEGINNERS Burton Hobson & Fred Reinfeld	2.00
_____CONCENTRATION—A Guide to Mental Mastery Mouni Sadhu	2.00
_____CONVERSATION MADE EASY Elliot Russell	1.00
_____CULPEPER'S HERBAL REMEDIES Dr. Nicholas Culpeper	2.00
_____CYBERNETICS WITHIN US Y. Saparina	3.00
_____DOCTOR PSYCHO-CYBERNETICS Maxwell Maltz, M.D.	2.50
_____DOG TRAINING MADE EASY & FUN John W. Kellogg	2.00
_____DREAMS & OMENS REVEALED Fred Gettings	2.00
_____DR. LINDNER'S SPECIAL WEIGHT CONTROL METHOD	1.00
_____DYNAMIC THINKING Melvin Powers	1.00
_____ENCYCLOPEDIA OF MODERN SEX &	
LOVE TECHNIQUES R. Macandrew	2.00
_____EXAM SECRET Dennis B. Jackson	1.00
_____EXTRASENSORY PERCEPTION Simeon Edmunds	2.00
_____FAST GOURMET COOKBOOK Poppy Cannon	2.50
_____FORTUNE TELLING WITH CARDS P. Foli	2.00
_____GAYELORD HAUSER'S NEW GUIDE TO INTELLIGENT REDUCING	3.00
_____GOULD'S GOLD & SILVER GUIDE TO COINS Maurice Gould	2.00
_____GREATEST POWER IN THE UNIVERSE U. S. Andersen	4.00

Melvin Powers
SELF-IMPROVEMENT
LIBRARY